HACKS FOR

PUBG

PLAYERS

ADVANCED STRATEGIES

HACKS FOR
PUBG
PLAYERS
ADVANCED
STRATEGIES

AN UNOFFICIAL GAMER'S GUIDE

JASON R. RICH

Racehorse Publishing

Copyright © 2019 by Hollan Publishing, Inc.

The PUBG (PlayerUnknown's Battlegrounds) game is copyright © Bluehole, Inc. and the PUBG Corporation.

Racehorse Publishing books may be purchased in bulk at special discounts for sales promotion, corporate gifts, fund-raising, or educational purposes. Special editions can also be created to specifications. For details, contact the Special Sales Department, 307 West 36th Street, 11th Floor, New York, NY 10018 or info@skyhorsepublishing.com.

Racehorse Publishing™ is a pending trademark of Skyhorse Publishing, Inc.®, a Delaware corporation.

Visit our website at www.skyhorsepublishing.com.

10 9 8 7 6 5 4 3 2 1

Library of Congress Cataloging-in-Publication Data is available on file.

Cover design by Brian Peterson
Cover photograph by Getty Images

Print ISBN: 978-1-63158-518-0
E-Book ISBN: 978-1-63158-520-3

Printed in the United States of America

CONTENTS

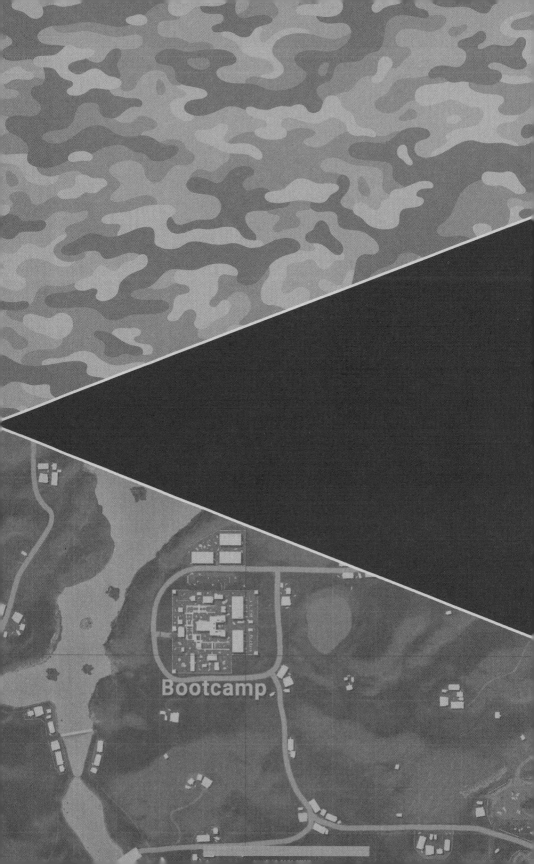

PREPARE TO KILL YOUR ADVERSARIES

Contrary to popular belief, your primary objective when experiencing an intense match in *PlayerUnknown's Battleground* (also known simply as *PUBG*) is *not* to kill as many enemy soldiers as possible (although, achieving those kills is certainly beneficial).

YOUR PRIMARY GOAL AS A GAMER SHOULD ALWAYS BE SURVIVAL! YOU WANT the soldier you're controlling to become the very last person alive on the island at the end of a match. Sounds easy, right? Well, it's definitely not!

DISCOVER WHAT *PUBG* IS ALL ABOUT

PUBG is a real-time, multiplayer, combat/adventure game that takes place on an island. Each gamer controls one soldier, who at the beginning of a match is armed only with their bare hands. There are several unique island maps where each match can take place.

While *PUBG* has been favorably compared to other mega-popular games, like *Fortnite: Battle Royale* and *Apex Legends*, this one has some significant differences. It definitely offers challenges and unique game-play experiences and features not offered by its competition.

Before each match, you have the opportunity to choose a game-play mode and map.

Game-play modes include **Solo**, **Duo**, and **Squad**. There's also the opportunity to create a **Custom** match, and then invite other gamers to experience it. By choosing the Custom match option, you're also able to participate in matches created by other gamers.

After choosing a game-play mode, up to 100 soldiers are transported to the pre-deployment area.

Everyone then boards an aircraft that'll take them directly over the island. You're not given a first-class airline ticket to travel on a luxury airline, however.

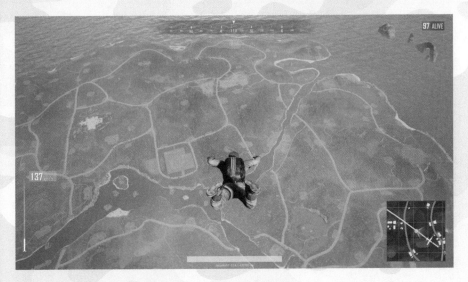

As soon as the island is reached, each soldier must leap from the aircraft and free fall toward land. A parachute is provided to ensure a safe landing.

DECIDE WHERE YOU'RE HEADED BEFORE LANDING

While in the pre-deployment area, or while riding in the aircraft, check the island map to view the random route the plane will take as it travels across the island. Use this information to help you choose the best time to leap from the plane and select what you believe is the ideal landing location.

Depending on your goals for a particular match, you can allow your soldier to free-fall at a steady pace toward land, and then simply wait for their parachute to deploy automatically. This strategy allows you to use the directional controls to glide through the air and cover a lot of territory across the island before landing, but it's not the fastest way to reach land. As a result, enemy soldiers could beat you to your desired landing spot and grab a weapon and ammo before you. If this happens, while you're still unarmed, you could be shot within moments after landing.

Getting killed during a match causes your soldier's immediate removal from that match. As you'll discover, in addition to getting shot or blown up by an enemy, there are many other ways to perish on the island. It's your responsibility to avoid all of them.

Many gamers opt to use their directional controls during free fall to speed up their soldier's descent to reach land faster. This helps to ensure that upon landing it'll be easier to find and grab weapons, ammo, and other useful items, so your soldier can defend themselves against enemies who land nearby.

Landing in a popular location on the map virtually guarantees that you'll encounter enemies almost immediately upon landing. This, of course, makes it harder to stay alive and gives you the added objective to find and grab a weapon quickly. As you're close to land, you'll see the parachutes of other nearby soldiers and be able to see where they're landing. If someone else is landing first, it's best to stay clear of that area until you've secured a weapon and ammo.

Choosing a more remote, less popular landing location typically means you will not encounter enemies right away. This gives you extra time to explore a bit, gather up an arsenal of weapons, ammo, items, and armor, and devise a plan to stay in the safe areas of the island, based on the location of the safe circle that's formed by the blue wall.

If you want to take your time during free fall after leaping from the plane, and maintain more navigational control while you're in midair, consider manually deploying your soldier's parachute anytime during free fall, as opposed to waiting for it to open automatically. The sooner you open the parachute, the more horizonal distance across the island you'll be able to travel, and the slower your soldier will descend.

Upon landing, your first objective is to find cover if there are enemies lurking around who may already be armed. Your second objective is to find and grab at least one weapon (and some compatible ammo) as quickly as possible, since upon landing, your soldier is unarmed and extremely vulnerable. In some cases, you may find armor first (shown on the left). In this case, the soldier discovered a Vest. Grab the armor and put it on for added protection. On the right, notice he's now wearing the vest.

Your best bet for finding a weapon and ammo is to enter into a nearby building or structure. You're apt to find weapons, ammo, loot items, armor, and/or health/boost -replenishment items lying out in the open, on the ground.

More often than not, you'll find compatible ammo for a weapon lying out in the open, next to a weapon. Be sure to grab the ammo also, and then immediately load the weapon so it's ready to shoot. Approach an item you want your soldier to grab and use the Pickup button or keyboard key to grab it and add it to your soldier's inventory.

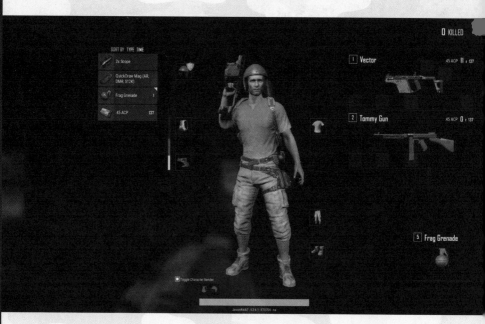

Once items are in your soldier's inventory, select one weapon at a time to use and then organize the inventory from your soldier's Inventory screen.

There are many types of guns available on the island. Each has a specialty. For example, a Pistol (shown here is the P1911) is an ideal close-range weapon.

When you have your soldier hold their breath and aim, they can steady their shot for additional accuracy. Notice the lungs icon to the right of the soldier's Health meter. This is the first-person viewing perspective for this weapon.

This is the normal aim for a Pistol that has no Weapon Attachments connected to it. This is the third-person shooting perspective for this weapon.

A Shotgun is best suited for close- or mid-range firefights. You can practice using this S12K Shotgun, just as you can every weapon, within *PUBG*'s Training Mode (shown here).

A Sniper Rifle or Designated Marksman Rifle (DMR), for example, is perfect for long-range shooting.

Shown here is a VSS Designated Marksman Rifle. On its own, it has a shooting range of 100 meters.

Any guns you manage to collect, such as this UMP9 Submachine Gun, are worthless without compatible ammunition. After collecting the correct type of ammunition for each gun your soldier is carrying, it's your responsibility to manually load the weapon and then reload it as needed, to ensure it's always ready to shoot should you encounter an unexpected enemy.

A gun without compatible ammo is worthless! As you'll discover from Section 4, "Collect and Manage Your Soldier's Arsenal," each gun can hold a predetermined amount of ammo at any given time, and each takes a different amount of time to reload. Running out of ammo during an intense firefight or having to wait too long to reload without having another loaded weapon on hand could easily become a deadly mistake.

If you try shooting an unloaded weapon, or you've run out of compatible ammo, a message that says, "There is no ammunition" will be displayed near the bottom-center of the screen (shown here).

Beyond collecting guns and ammo, through exploration, by killing enemies, and by approaching Supply Drops (shown here), you can collect a vast assortment of Weapon Attachments. These are items that attach to specific types of guns to increase their capabilities, aiming accuracy, bullet capacity, and power. Once you find and collect Weapon Attachments, from the Inventory screen, manually move them, one at a time, from your soldier's inventory and attach each to a compatible weapon in order to take advantage of it.

Collecting and attaching the best combination of Weapon Attachments to the guns you have on hand is one of the core strategies that'll help you achieve more kills during a match and stay alive longer. A Red Dot Sight is an example of a useful Weapon Attachment that makes a compatible weapon easier and faster to accurately aim.

After you've picked up a Weapon Attachment, access your soldier's Inventory screen. Initially, the Weapon Attachments you pick up will appear on the left side of the screen, in the column that shows what your soldier is currently holding. Drag a Weapon Attachment icon to the right side of the screen and place it into a box displayed near one of your compatible weapons. Here, the Red Dot Sight has been attached to a UMP9 Submachine Gun.

This is the UMP9 with the Red Dot Sight being aimed. If you look closely, you'll see the red dot in the dead center of the weapon's crosshair. Point the red dot at your target and pull the trigger to ensure a direct hit.

There are also an assortment of other weapons, besides guns, that can be used to distract, injure, confuse, or potentially kill enemies. Various types of grenades are an example of these weapons. Here, a Frag Grenade (an explosive type of grenade) is about to be picked up and added to the soldier's inventory. As you can see, a message is also displayed stating that in 30 seconds, the blue wall will move and the safe area of the island will soon shrink. This should be a reminder to check the island map to ensure you're positioned within the safe area. If not, you'd better get moving!

Before any match, you have the ability to customize the appearance of your soldier. How to do this is explained within Section 2, "Ways to Customize Your Soldier's Appearance." These customizations are for cosmetic purposes only! Anything you choose for your soldier to wear before a match will not provide any tactical advantage. (The one exception to this is a full bodysuit, like the Snow suit, which is shown here. These suits can help your soldier blend in with their surroundings and serve as camouflage in specific types of terrain.)

Once a match begins, collect armor for your soldier to provide additional protection. *PUBG* offers two main types of armor–Helmets and Vests. To increase the amount of stuff your soldier can carry in their inventory, it's also useful to collect and wear a Backpack. At the start of a match, you'll typically find level 1 armor. However, as the match progresses, you can always upgrade your armor. Here, the soldier is about to upgrade to a level 2 Helmet.

There are three levels of Helmets, Vests, and Backpacks. A level 3 Helmet or Vest offers more protection than a level 1 or level 2 Helmet or Vest. Likewise, a level 3 Backpack (shown here) holds more content than a level 1 or level 2 Backpack. Level 3 Helmets, Vests, and Backpacks are much harder to come across on the island. You typically need to obtain them from a Supply Drop or by killing enemies during the mid to late stages of a match.

WAYS TO STAY ALIVE LONGER

There are many strategies you'll soon learn to help you stay alive longer during a match. One is to take full advantage of the Health and Boost items that can be collected and used during your stay on the island.

At the start of a match, your soldier's Health meter is at 100 percent, and their Boost meter is at zero. Each time a soldier gets injured, some of their Health diminishes. When their Health meter reaches zero, they're dead. Here, the soldier was just shot and his Health meter quickly decreased to zero, so he was eliminated.

Various items, like Med Kits, First Aid Kits (shown on the left), and Bandages (shown on the right) can be picked up, stored in a soldier's inventory, and then used to replenish some or all of their health. You'll learn more about these within Section 6, "Find and Use the Best Armor- and Health-Related Items."

Your soldier's Health meter is always displayed near the bottom-center of the screen on most gaming platforms. Displayed directly above it is your soldier's Boost meter. Using items like Energy Drinks, it's possible to increase your soldier's Boost meter, which can allow them to temporarily move and heal faster.

THERE'S MORE TO WORRY ABOUT ON THE ISLAND THAN ENEMIES

In addition to being shot at or blown up by enemy soldiers, there are a bunch of other dangers on the island, including the blue wall and Red Zone. At the start of each match, the entire island is safe to travel around. That all changes when the deadly blue wall starts to move in. Here, the soldier is on the safe side, but right up against the blue wall.

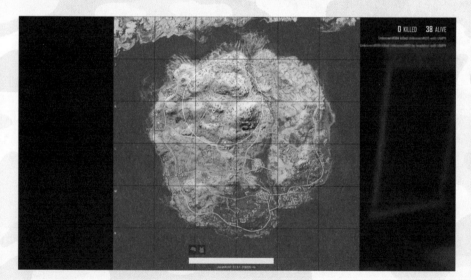

Shortly after each match begins, the blue wall forms and begins to close in around the island, forming a circle within which is the safe zone. Everything outside of the blue wall becomes a deadly place for your soldier to be. For every second your soldier spends on the wrong side of the blue wall, some of their health gets depleted. Shown here is the island map partway through a match. As you can see, much of the area is no longer safe (and displayed in blue). The current safe area is within the larger circle, and the inner white circle shows where the safe area will be once the blue wall moves again.

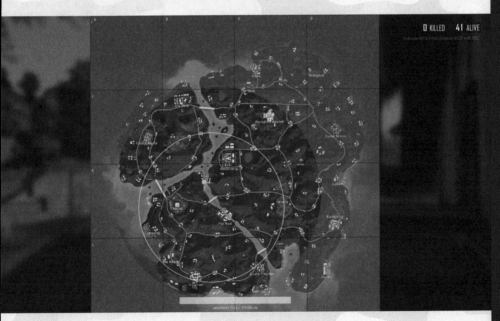

Every few minutes, the blue wall shrinks the size of the safe area on the island. By consulting the island map or the mini-map displayed on the main game screen, you're able to determine where the safe area of the island is currently located, as well as where the blue wall will be moving to next. During the End Game (the final minutes of a match), the entire safe area can be seen within the mini-map that's continuously displayed in the bottom-right corner of the main game screen (when playing the PC version of *PUBG*). Its location may vary, based on which gaming system you're using.

Thanks to the blue wall, each time the safe circle shrinks, this forces all of the surviving soldiers on the island to move into a more confined space. Doing this increases the danger from enemy attacks and makes it more likely that your soldier will be forced to fight in order to stay alive.

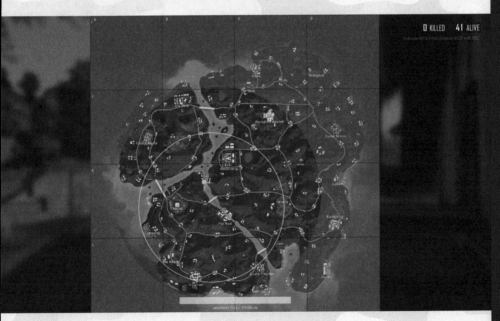

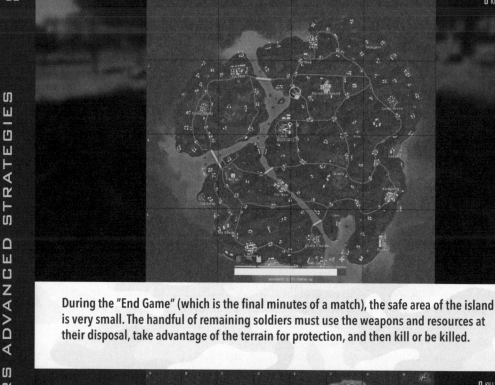

During the "End Game" (which is the final minutes of a match), the safe area of the island is very small. The handful of remaining soldiers must use the weapons and resources at their disposal, take advantage of the terrain for protection, and then kill or be killed.

Somewhere on the island, every match also has a Red Zone. This is a random area that is depicted as a red circle on the island map. This area gets bombed, so if your soldier gets stuck within it, he or she must take cover within a building to remain safe or leave the area as quickly as possible.

Your soldier can walk or run to travel around the island. Anytime they're out in the open, however, it's never a good idea to travel in a straight line. Using objects in the terrain, such as buildings, trees, or rocks for cover, run (don't walk) in a zigzag and unpredictable pattern to avoid being an easy target for your enemies.

When the need arises, your soldier can crouch down.

Sometimes, it makes sense for your soldier to lie down on the ground and/or crawl to avoid being seen or to become a harder target to hit.

Your soldier can climb onto or over objects as needed and can jump up or across objects as well. For example, by crouching down and jumping, soldiers can enter into some structures through a window, as opposed to walking through an open doorway.

One way to cross bodies of water is to swim. Your soldier can swim along the top of the water.

A soldier can also dive down and swim underwater to avoid being seen. Periodically, a submerged soldier will need to return to the surface for air. Notice the lungs icon displayed to the right of the soldier's Health meter. When the lungs icon turns solid red, your soldier will drown.

Scattered throughout the island are a collection of vehicles that can be driven. If you're playing a Duo or Squad match, your soldier can either drive a vehicle or become a passenger while a teammate or squad mate is driving.

Vehicles allow your soldier to travel around the island much faster than walking or running. Each type of vehicle, however, is better suited to help you cross a specific type of terrain. For example, a Buggy is the perfect all-terrain vehicle for traveling off of paved roads and across rugged terrain that includes hills and mountains.

A motorcycle is often faster and much more maneuverable that most full-size sedans, vans, or trucks, for example.

A snowmobile is idea for traveling across ice or snow, while a Jet Ski or boat makes it easier and faster to travel across large bodies of water. When possible, choose the best type of vehicle for the terrain you're currently in, keeping in mind where you're trying to go and what types of obstacles you may encounter along the way.

Just like in real life, vehicles run on gas. If you're the first person to discover and commandeer a vehicle during a match, its gas tank should start off full. However, by driving the vehicle yourself, or if it's already been driven during a match, chances are you'll need to refill the vehicle's gas tank. This is done using Gas Cans that can be found, collected, and stored within your soldier's inventory until they're needed.

A vehicle without gas can't be driven, but it can still be used to hide behind (or within) for cover if you're being attacked. When hiding behind a vehicle you don't plan on driving in the future, shoot or punch out the tires to lower the vehicle. Doing this will offer more protection and prevent a sharp-shooter from injuring your soldier by shooting under the vehicle your soldier is hiding behind. Of course, already disabled vehicles also provide excellent cover. This is shown here on an iPad Pro.

Using a gun, it's possible to disable most moving vehicles or ones that are standing still by destroying two or more of its tires. Punching out tires makes less noise than shooting them with a gun. Generating as little noise as possible is typically beneficial if you want to keep enemies from determining your location.

Vehicles that offer a roof offer better protection against incoming gun attacks, while those without roofs tend to be able to travel at faster speeds and can often be more maneuverable (making it easier to outrun an enemy attack). Check out Section 6, "Quickly and Safely Navigate Around," for tips on driving or riding in *PUBG*'s various types of vehicles.

LISTEN UP! SOUND PLAYS AN ESSENTIAL ROLE IN *PUBG*

All of the sound effects incorporated into *PUBG* play an important role in the game. Thus, it's an excellent idea to wear good-quality headphones when playing. From the game's **Settings** menu, choose the **Audio** submenu and turn down the **Music** volume, but turn up the **Effects** levels.

If you'll be playing Duo or Squad matches, you'll definitely want to use a gaming headset. This allows you to hear all of the sound effects, plus talk to your partner or squad mates in real time during each match. The importance of being able to communicate with your allies to coordinate well-planned attacks or defensive maneuvers can't be emphasized enough.

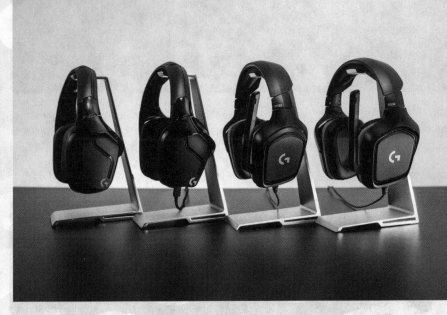

Many companies now offer wireless and corded gaming headsets with a built-in microphone and surround sound audio. Shown here are some of the popular Logitech G gaming headsets (www.logitechg.com), which range in price from $59.99 (US) to $139.99 (US). These are compatible with PCs and all popular console-based gaming systems.

HyperX (www.hyperxgaming.com/us/headsets), Razer (www.razer.com/gaming-headsets-and-audio), and Turtle Beach Corp. (www.turtlebeach.com) are three other gaming headset manufacturers used by the top-ranked gamers.

Everything a soldier does in the game generates noise. The more noise your soldier makes, the easier it'll be for enemies to pinpoint their location and launch an attack. Footsteps from a soldier created while they're walking or running generate sound that intensifies the closer you are to them.

Opening and closing doors, using a weapon or item, and riding in a vehicle also generate noise that can be heard by nearby enemies. Regardless of where you are or what you're doing, it's to your advantage to make the least amount of noise possible.

Prior to a match, take off your soldier's shoes. You'll be able to walk or run at the same speed as when your soldier is wearing shoes, but he or she will generate less noise when moving around. From the Customize Feet screen (shown here), unselect whatever shoes your soldier is wearing, so he's barefoot. The difference in volume of footsteps when wearing shoes versus going barefoot has less of an impact now than it did in the past, but it's still something to consider if you want to travel around and potentially go unheard by your nearby enemies.

Keep in mind, soldiers generate different types of sound depending on the terrain they're in. Get to know the different types of sounds, so you can more easily identify where your enemies are located, what they're doing, and their distance from your soldier, simply by the noises they make.

PUBG has more than nine types of terrain, and when a soldier travels along each type of terrain, a different sound is created. Terrain types include: concrete, wood, metal, sand, carpet, stairs, grass, water, and paved roads.

Remember, sounds will be louder the closer you are to your enemies. You'll also be able to tell, if you listen carefully, from which direction the sounds are coming from, including if they're emanating from above or below your soldier's location, so pay attention.

Some terrain sounds are very similar but being able to differentiate between them can help you determine from which direction an enemy is approaching. Being able to identify sound effects clearly is one of the main reasons why you should play *PUBG* with quality headphones or a gaming headset.

USE A GAMING KEYBOARD/MOUSE OR A GOOD-QUALITY CONTROLLER

By default, *PUBG* is set up so Windows PC users can use their keyboard and mouse to control all of their soldier's actions during a match.

For some gamers, a keyboard/mouse combo offers the most precise and responsive control options, especially if you're using a specialty gaming keyboard and mouse, such as those offered by Corsair (www.corsair.com), Logitech (www.logitechg.com), or Razer www.razer.com/gaming-keyboards). The Razer Huntsman Elite WR (2018) for the PC ($199.99) is shown here.

It's also possible for PC gamers to connect an Xbox One controller to their PC and then use the controller alone (or in conjunction with their keyboard/mouse) to control everything in the game. A wireless or corded Xbox One controller can be used.

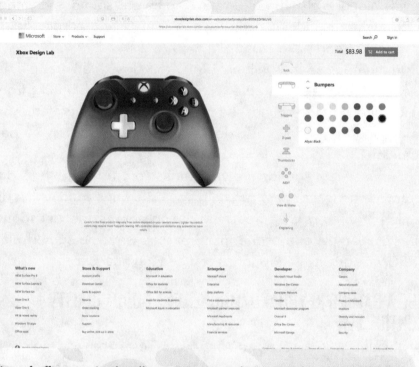

Microsoft offers a service that allows you to custom design a wireless or corded Xbox One controller. These controllers look different cosmetically but offer the same functionality as the controller that comes with the gaming system. The price varies, based on options you choose. Check out https://xboxdesignlab.xbox.com/en-us to learn more about this option.

Offering more precision that a standard console controller, several companies, such as SCUF Gaming (www.scufgaming.com), manufacture specialty Xbox One and PS4 controllers designed to cater to the needs of advanced gamers. The SCUF Impact controller for the PS4 ($139.95 US) is shown here.

Some believe these specialized controllers provide a slight advantage when playing *PUBG*, because they offer added precision and better response time, but this is mostly a matter of personal preference.

Xbox One or PS4 console–based gamers can use the standard wireless controllers that came bundled with their gaming system, or upgrade to more advanced controllers. It's also possible to connect a gaming keyboard and mouse directly to a console-based system. The Turret for Xbox One gaming keyboard and mouse ($249.99 US) from Razer is shown here.

THERE ARE OPTIONAL CONTROLLERS FOR MOBILE DEVICES TOO

PUBG Mobile takes advantage of the touchscreen on your smartphone or tablet to control the on-screen action. However, there are third-party controller options that can be used in conjunction with an iPhone, iPad, or Android-based mobile device. Shown here is *PUBG Mobile* (also known as *PUBGM*) on an iPad Pro.

There are also specialty controller options available for smartphones and tablets that provide better control over *PUBG* than what's offered when using the default touchscreen controls. Check out companies like GameSir (www.gamesir.hk) and GameVice (https://gamevice.com/collections/mobile-console-gaming) to learn more about these optional controllers. The GameVice controller for iPhone ($79.95) is shown here.

MEMORIZE THE CONTROLS

Regardless of whether you're using a keyboard/mouse combo or a controller, prior to a match, you're able to choose a game controller layout or customize your keyboard and mouse layout (key bindings). Once you make the customizations you deem necessary, memorize which button or key corresponds with each command or control.

KEY GUIDE
DEFAULT SETTINGS

COMMON ACTIONS

Move	W A S D	Free Look	L ALT +
Jump / Vault	SPACE BAR	Sprint	L SHIFT
Interact	F	Inventory	TAB I

Crouch	C	Prone	Z
Walk	L CTRL	Auto Run	=
Map	M		

COMBAT ACTIONS

Fire		Aim (HOLD)	
Toggle Fire Mode	B	Peek Left / Right	Q E

ADS (CLICK)		Reload	R
Select Weapon	1 ~ 5	Unarm	X

PUBG

In addition to memorizing the main controls for moving your soldier around, as well as aiming, reloading, and firing your weapon(s), it's important to practice using the subtle motions your soldier is capable of, so you understand exactly how to jump, climb, crawl, swim, drive a vehicle, and use Health items. For example, you're able to free-look around your soldier. On a PC, this is done by holding down the ALT key while moving the mouse. Shown here are the default key bindings for the PC version of *PUBG*.

While aiming a weapon, have your soldier hold their breath when pulling the trigger to improve their accuracy. On a PC, this is done by holding the Shift key while aiming. Upon doing this, you'll be able to virtually zoom in slightly to your target, even without attaching an optional scope to the weapon. Keep in mind, your soldier can only hold their breath for so long. If he or she runs out of air while aiming, it'll take several seconds to recover. Notice the lungs icon that's displayed to the immediate right of the Health meter.

Another subtle, but useful action is to tip-toe, as opposed to walk. This causes your soldier to move slower, but it generates much less noise from footsteps. On a PC, for example, press the Ctrl key while walking to tiptoe instead.

Wasting even a fraction of second figuring out which button or key to press in order to complete an action during a battle could easily lead to your soldier's quick death.

SETTINGS

| GRAPHICS | CONTROL | SOUND | GAMEPLAY |

15X Scope Sensitivity

COMMON

Move Forward	W
Move Backward	S
Strafe Right	D
Strafe Left	A
Walk / Glide	Left Ctrl
Sprint / Fast Descent	Left Shift
Jump / Vault	Space Bar
Jump Only	
Vault Only	
Crouch	C
Prone	Z

CLOSE   DEFAULT   APPLY

If you're a *PUBG* newb, leave the controller or keyboard/mouse settings and key bindings at their default settings. Then, once you're more acquainted with the game, make customizations that could potentially improve your soldier's overall speed, reaction time, and aiming/shooting accuracy. Notice the option (displayed in the bottom-left corner of the screen) that allows you to return to the Default settings.

During a match, it's easy to switch between a first- and third-person viewing perspective. While using the third-person perspective, if you right-click the mouse (on a PC) while carrying a gun, this gives you a view looking down the sight of the weapon. Holding down the right mouse button switches to an over-the-shoulder view. Shown on the left is first-person perspective (FPP). Shown on the right is third-person perspective (TPP).

While hiding behind a solid barrier and using it as a shield, one subtle move that can save your life by not making your soldier's entire body visible and vulnerable is to lean out from behind the cover to see where your enemies are or to shoot, for example.

Here, the soldier is hiding behind a solid wall near a doorway and peeking out to the right with his gun drawn.

The soldier has moved to the opposite side of the doorway and is now peeking out to the left with his gun drawn.

A FAST INTERNET CONNECTION IS ESSENTIAL WHEN PLAYING *PUBG*

SETTINGS

| GRAPHICS | CONTROL | SOUND | GAMEPLAY |

LANGUAGE

Language Setting — English

VIDEO CAPTURE

Highlights Auto Capture — Disable

DISPLAY SETTINGS

Display Mode — Fullscreen (Windowed)

Resolution — 1920 * 1080

FPP Camera FOV

Brightness

Lobby FPS Limit — Unlimited

In-Game FPS Limit — Unlimited

Smoothed Frame Rate

ADVANCED SETTINGS

Overall Quality — Custom

CLOSE   DEFAULT   APPLY

When playing the PC or console version of *PUBG*, for example, if you have a slower Internet connection, you'll benefit from reducing the display resolution of the game from the Settings menu.

Highlight and select the Graphics submenu tab, and then adjust each option, based on the equipment you're using and the level of detail you want to see. If you know you have a slower Internet connection and/or a lower-end computer, you'll benefit from reducing the resolution and quality of the graphics generated by the game.

While the graphics won't look as awesome in a lower resolution, the speed of the game and your soldier's reaction time will improve. If you have the game set at high resolution and you attempt to lie down in a grassy area, for example, thinking it'll provide camouflage and keep you out of your enemy's sights, you could be in for a bad surprise.

When your adversary has their resolution set lower, the detail of the grassy area won't be as detailed, and your soldier will sometimes appear as if he or she is simply lying on the ground, out in the open. Giving up more detailed graphics in favor of faster reaction time will often serve you well during a match.

When choosing your Region, select the one you're actually in to achieve the fastest connection to the game's servers. If you want to challenge yourself against players from a different region, you have the option of choosing an alternate region, but your connection to that *PUBG* servers will likely be slower.

CONSIDER AN ETHERNET CONNECTION TO THE INTERNET

Windows PC and console-based systems have the ability to connect to the Internet via a wireless (Wi-Fi) connection or using a physical Ethernet cable that connects between your computer and modem (or a router). A wired connection is sometimes more reliable and faster than wireless connection, and the improved speed could positively impact your game-play.

For computers that don't have an Ethernet port built-in, an inexpensive Ethernet adapter can be purchased online or from popular consumer electronics stores. The Xbox One and PS4 both have Ethernet ports built into the systems, but a standard Ethernet cable (they come in many different lengths) needs to be purchased separately.

HOW TO PURCHASE AND DOWNLOAD THE LATEST VERSION OF THE GAME

Regardless of which gaming platform you use to experience *PUBG*, the actual game-play is very similar, although as you'll soon discover, how the game screen looks varies slightly in each version. While games like *Fortnite: Battle Royale* and *Apex Legends* are free but have in-game purchases, it's necessary to purchase the core *PUBG* game, and then if you choose, also make in-game purchases.

The retail price of the game varies, but for the core game, plan on spending about $30.00 (US) for the PC, PS4, or Xbox One version. The mobile version of *PUBG* is free, but in-app purchases are required to acquire a Season Pass and other game content. Throughout this strategy guide, most of the screenshots were taken using the PC version of the game.

A retail version of *PUBG* is sold in stores that sell computer and video games, however, once you purchase the game at your favorite store, you'll still need to download and install the entire game via the Internet, as updated versions of *PUBG* are released on a regular basis.

The retail versions typically include a bundle of additional content, such as a Season Pass, Crates, Items, and in-game currency that can be used to acquire additional items. The alternative is to purchase the game online and then download it directly to your computer or console-based system.

To purchase the PC version of the game, launch your favorite web browser and visit **www .pubg.com**. Click on the **Buy Now** button that's displayed in the top-right corner of the screen. You'll be able to purchase the core game, or a bundle pack that includes a Season Pass or a Season Pass along with downloadable content for the game.

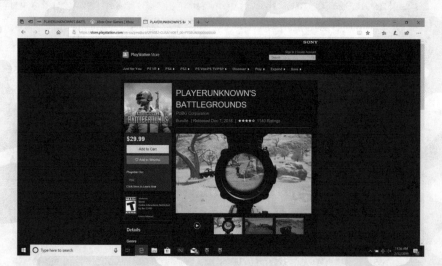

The PlayStation 4 version is available from the **PlayStation Store** (https://store .playstation.com/en-us/product/UP5082-CUSA14081_00-PTSBUN0000000000).

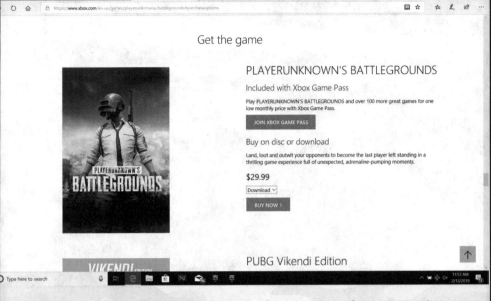

The Xbox One version of *PUBG* is available online from the **Microsoft Store** (www.xbox .com/en-US/games/playerunknowns-battlegrounds#purchaseoptions).

The iOS (iPhone/iPad) version of **PUBG Mobile** is available from the **App Store**, and the Android-based version of the game can be purchased and acquired from the **Google Play Store**. For more information about *PUBG Mobile*, visit **www.pubgmobile .com**.

EVERY GAMING SEASON, EXPECT SOME MAJOR CHANGES

In order to keep *PUBG* exciting and fresh over time, PlayerUn-known regularly updates the game with new island maps, along with new weapons, items, and vehicles, for example. At the same time, existing island maps get tweaked, existing points of interest (locations) get modified, and new types of terrain are periodically introduced.

PREPARE TO KILL YOUR ADVERSARIES

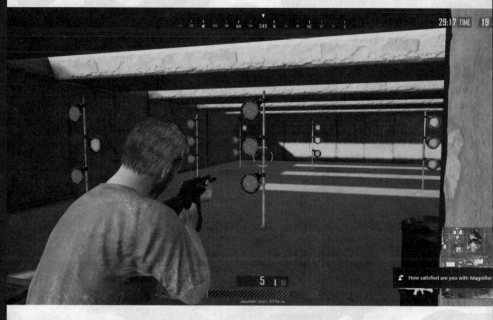

As new weapons are introduced into the game, take the time to use Training mode and discover how to best utilize each new weapon firsthand, before needing to use it in matches during life and death battles. Becoming comfortable using a broad range of weapons definitely gives you an advantage when playing *PUBG*, since you'll experience combat situations in many different types of terrain.

Knowing how and when to use the best close-range, mid-range, and long-range guns, as well as different types of throwable grenades will make it much easier to keep your soldier alive and be victorious when engaged in firefights.

Understanding how to upgrade weapons using Weapon Attachments is also a valuable *PUBG* skill to master early on, since using Weapon Attachments can improve a gun's aiming accuracy, ammunition capacity, and firing rate, for example.

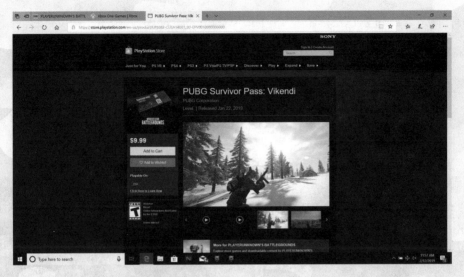

In addition to purchasing the *PUBG* game itself, every 10 weeks or so, you have the option to buy a new Survivor Pass (also referred to as an Event Pass). They cost around $10.00 (US) each. Once an Event Pass is activated, you're able to participate in optional in-game Missions. Completing these missions allows you to earn clothing items and other items for your soldier that are used to customize his or her appearance. Whether or not you purchase an Event Pass is optional.

UNDERSTANDING *PUBG* IS ONLY THE FIRST STEP

PUBG Hacks: Advanced Strategies will help you better understand all of the nuances of *PUBG*, plus discover many useful game-play tips and strategies that'll help you stay alive longer, achieve more kills, and ultimately win more matches.

However, just reading this book is not enough. Becoming a highly skilled *PUBG* player is going to take practice . . . a lot of practice!

As you're about to discover, survival during a match requires you to handle a wide range of tasks simultaneously, some of which include:

- Safely explore the island—including within all sorts of structures and buildings.
- Find and gather useful weapons, ammo, armor, and items.

- Maintain your soldier's health, especially if he's injured from an attack.
- Avoid the blue wall and the Red Zone.
- Travel around the island on foot or by driving a vehicle.
- Utilize the terrain surrounding your soldier to your advantage.
- Avoid ambushes and traps set by your enemies.
- Anticipate what your opponents will do, and quickly develop strategies to outsmart them.
- Attack and kill your adversaries.

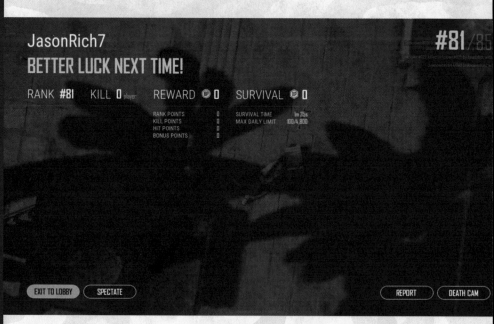

Each time you get killed, instead of immediately returning to the Lobby and entering into a new match, take advantage of Spectator mode. This allows you to watch the rest of the match you were just eliminated from. By watching other gamers, particularly in the final stages of a match, you can discover useful strategies and fighting techniques, plus get to know the island's terrain a bit better, while discovering where useful items are likely to be found during future matches. To enter into Spectator mode, from the Better Luck Next Time screen, choose the Spectate option that's displayed near the bottom-left corner of the screen.

After memorizing the controls, focus on developing your muscle memory (which takes plenty of repetition and practice), so you can focus your attention on developing strategies to kill off your opponents in the combat situations you're facing, as opposed to wasting time figuring out which keyboard/mouse or controller button to press.

Even once you know the secrets that'll help you become a better *PUBG* gamer, expect that you're going to be killed a lot more often than you're going to win matches. There's always going to be other players who are more experienced, who react faster than you, or who simply get lucky during a match.

Early on, instead of trying to win matches and get frustrated in the process, focus on staying alive within matches longer by fine-tuning your exploration and survival skills, while working to improve your kill count during each match. Keep your priorities straight as you progress through a match, without letting your emotions or taunts from your adversaries get the best of you.

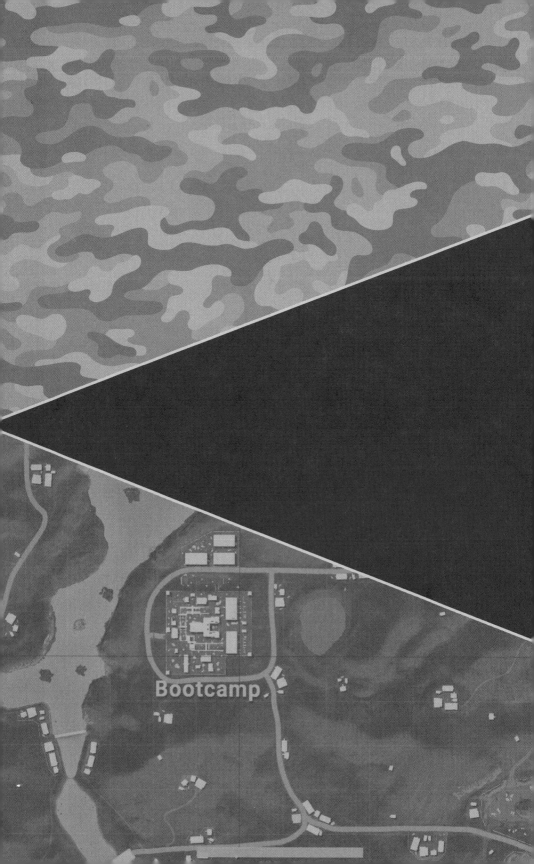

SECTION 2

WAYS TO CUSTOMIZE YOUR SOLDIER'S APPEARANCE

EVERY GAMER WHO PARTICIPATES IN *PUBG* MATCHES HAS A UNIQUE SET OF skills and experiences that they bring into each battle. This can include experience playing other combat-oriented games. After playing *PUBG* for a bit, most gamers become proficient using certain weapons, and pick their favorite go-to weapons when encountering specific combat scenarios. Gamers also react to various situations very differently.

Without studying your competition during matches, it's very difficult to anticipate what their actions will be when confronted with life or death situations, when everyone is making split-second decisions.

Thus, to become a skilled and successful *PUBG* gamer, develop the ability to react very quickly to the offensive and defensive strategies used by your adversaries, keeping in mind that those you're fighting against will often surprise you. Expect other gamers to act unpredictably either as part of their planned fighting strategies, or out of pure panic and the inability to think clearly during intense battles.

With up to 99 other gamers experiencing the same match as you, some personalities will shine as skilled players quickly kill off enemies, while others will shy away from conflict and approach challenges and obstacles very differently. It's this diversity amongst gamers that makes every match both exciting and unique.

To ensure that each gamer gets to showcase their gaming skills, as well as their unique personality and flare for fashion, *PUBG* offers many ways to customize the appearance of your soldier.

From the Lobby screen before a match, select the Customize option to adjust your soldier's appearance, keeping in mind that everything you do here is for cosmetic purposes only.

Just like in real life, first impressions make an impact on what others think. If your soldier is wearing items that are rare, expensive, limited edition, or difficult to acquire, this immediately implies to your competition that you've invested a lot of time, effort, and money playing *PUBG*, and you're likely a formidable opponent.

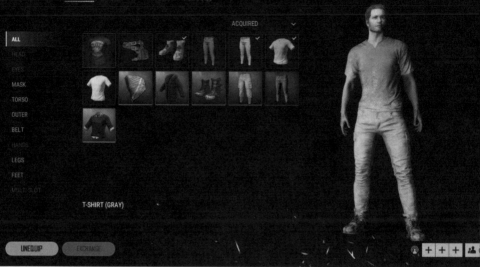

When a soldier is dressed in just a basic T-shirt and pants, chosen from the core selection of items that come bundled with *PUBG*, this could announce to everyone who sees your soldier in the game that you're an inexperienced noob, which to an experienced gamer, translates to an easy kill and makes you a potential target.

Don't be fooled by appearances, however. A noob can spend extra money to dress their soldier in expensive items, and/or pay to complete levels and unlock otherwise difficult to acquire items without completing missions or challenges to get them. Hence, a noob's soldier might give off a vibe that implies experience and skill, when in reality, the gamer will be very easy to defeat during a firefight.

Meanwhile, experienced *PUBG* gamers can dress down their soldier, dressing him or her in only default items, to give off the appearance of a noob. This often provides adversaries with a false sense of superiority during firefights. Thus, an experienced gamer can "act" and look like a noob to give their enemies a false sense of confidence before killing them using highly advanced weapons and fighting skills.

PERSONALIZE YOUR SOLDIER'S APPEARANCE

Prior to a match, select the Customize option, followed by the Appearance option, to define what your soldier will look like. The four main Appearance categories include Sex, Skin Color/Ethnicity, Hair, and Makeup.

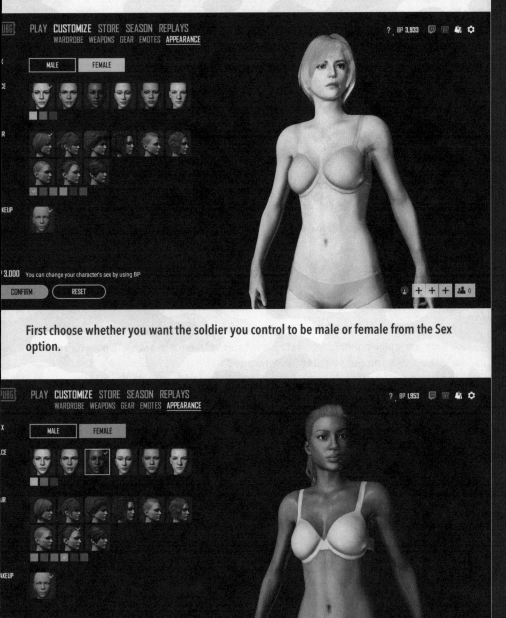

First choose whether you want the soldier you control to be male or female from the Sex option.

Next, from the Face option, choose your soldier's ethnicity and skin color. Select a face from the displayed thumbnails, and then click on one of the skin color options.

Click on any of the hairstyle icons displayed in conjunction with the Hair heading. When you first start playing *PUBG*, at least nine different styles are available. Once you've selected a style, choose a desired hair color.

Unless you purchase or unlock Makeup options, none are initially available to you. A Makeup option allows a male or female soldier to disguise their face using themed makeup.

By mixing and matching the different Appearance, Wardrobe, Weapons, and Gear options available from the Customize menu, it's possible to make your soldier look truly unique. The possible combinations are in the millions, and with additional items continuously being added to the game, there are always fun and interesting new ways to alter your soldier's appearance.

HOW TO CUSTOMIZE YOUR SOLDIER'S OUTFIT

After selecting the Customize option from *PUBG*'s main menu, you'll discover a submenu that allows you to choose your soldier's Wardrobe, Weapons, Gear, Emotes, and Appearance. Even if this is your first time playing *PUBG*, a selection of choices is provided, although you can purchase an ever changing selection of additional items from the Store, or unlock them during game-play, for example.

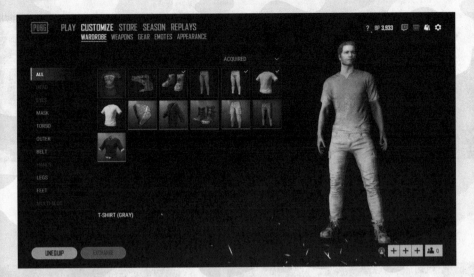

Select the Wardrobe option, and then select the All option on the left side of the Wardrobe screen (shown here on a PC), to see all of the items available for customizing what your soldier will wear. Once you acquire or unlock more items, you can easily sort them by clicking on or selecting the Head, Eyes, Mask, Torso, Outer, Belt, Hands, Legs, Feet, or Multi-Slot submenu option.

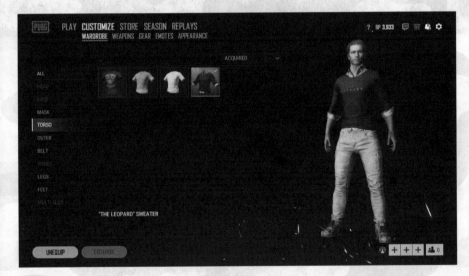

Select the Torso option, for example, to view available shirts. Remember, none of the items you use to dress your soldier impact your soldier's abilities in any way during a match. You're simply able to give your soldier a unique appearance. That being said, dressing your soldier in brightly colored items will make him or her stand out more on the island, potentially making them easier to spot and target. Dressing in dark or camouflage color schemes will make it easier for your soldier to blend into his or her surroundings.

After you play *PUBG* for a while and unlock items, select the Weapons and Gear submenu options to choose more ways to customize the appearance of your soldier. As a noob, no items in these categories are immediately available to you. Again, what you choose here is for cosmetic purposes only.

While looking at the Customize Wardrobe screen, you can select one item at a time that you already own and sell it back to the Shop in exchange for BP (in game currency). Not all items can be exchanged, however. If the item can be exchanged, the Exchange button near the bottom-left corner of the screen will become active. Click on it to see how much the item is worth, and then decide if you want to sell. Click OK to sell or Cancel to abort the sale. If you sell an item, you're then able to use the BP to purchase other items from the Shop.

SHOWCASE YOUR SOLDIER'S PERSONALITY WITH EMOTES

Emotes are movements that allow you to taunt and communicate with your enemies without speaking to them. Anytime you use an Emote during a match, all soldiers in the immediate area will see it.

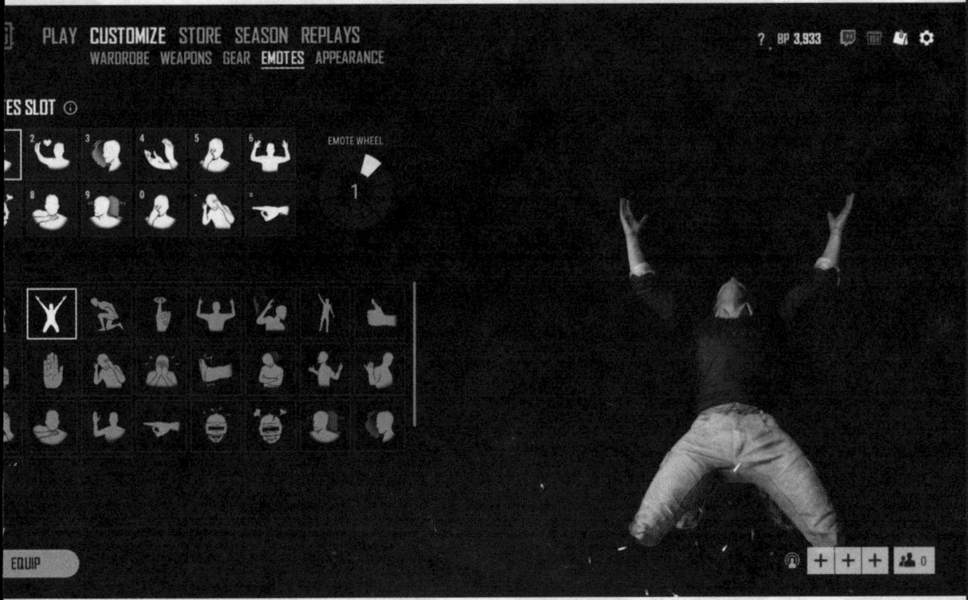

Some gamers use Emotes to communicate nonverbally with their partner or squad mates when playing a Duo or Squad match. You can also use Emotes to taunt an enemy or brag after making a kill, for example.

Select the Emotes option from the Customize menu and choose up to 12 different emotes that you'd like your soldier to be able to use during a match. Initially, *PUBG* offers 21 different Emotes to choose from. However, many more can be acquired and unlocked as you play.

One at a time, select an Emotes Slot displayed near the top of the screen, and then choose one Emote from the Emote icons near the bottom of the screen to place within each slot. Click on the Equip button to add it to your soldier's Emote Wheel. As you select an Emote, a preview of what it looks like is displayed on the right side of the screen.

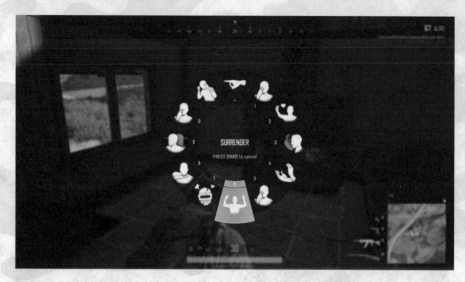

After choosing the 12 Emotes you want available during a match, the Emote Wheel will be full. Then, anytime during a match (or while in the pre-deployment area before a match), access the Emote Wheel and choose which Emote you want to showcase.

Until you've mastered fighting and survival skills that allow you to win firefights and stay alive during matches, don't worry too much about Emotes. Aside from potentially being used to lure, distract, or attract the attention of enemies, for example, Emotes give you little tactical advantage.

WAYS TO ACQUIRE MORE ITEMS

Additional items are continuously being added to the game. Some can be purchased from the Store using real money. From the game's main menu, click on the Store option, followed by the Items option.

DRAGON PRINT TANG (RED)

$4.99   BACK

Some items can be purchased individually. Prices are displayed below each item offered in the Store.

EAST ERANGEL POLICE CRATE

QUANTITY	1
PRICE	BP1,200
TOTAL	BP1,200

This set contains one or more items that you already own. Duplicate items will not be refunded. Are you sure you wish to purchase?

CONFIRM   CANCEL

Crates can be purchased for slightly more money from within the Store. A Crate includes a collection of items that can be purchased at once, often for a discounted price (compared to buying items separately).

Once you acquire a Crate, a special key is sometimes needed to open it. The correct key (if one is needed) can be unlocked within the game or purchased. Once a Crate is opened, the item(s) within it will be displayed and added to your soldier's Inventory.

Certain Keys can be purchased separately, others get acquired by completing missions. These allow you to customize the appearance of weapons you find and grab during each match. While using a Key changes how a weapon looks, these do not impact how a weapon functions.

Additional Emotes can also be purchased, one at a time, by selecting the Store option, followed by the Emotes option.

As you play *PUBG*, your soldier gains Experience Points and will improve their level. Upon achieving specific level milestones, additional items get unlocked as prizes. However, instead of actually achieving those milestones, it's possible to buy and unlock 5 ($4.99 US), 20 ($17.99 US), or 50 ($34.99 US) levels at a time, and immediately acquire the prize items associated with achieving those level milestones without having to do anything but spend real money.

In addition to shopping from the Store to acquire Items, Steam (the online server that hosts *PUBG* for Windows PC gamers) hosts the Community Market. This allows players to buy and sell items. This is the perfect place to acquire a rare or discontinued item, or quickly purchase an item that's not currently available from the Store. Some items are sold at a discount, while for rare items, you may have to pay a premium to purchase it from another gamer, as opposed to from the PlayerUnknown Shop.

Select an item from the Community Market, and then choose whether you want to Purchase or Sell it. As you'll discover, items, Crates, and Keys, for example, are priced anywhere from a few cents each (US), up to hundreds of dollars, so shop wisely.

PlayerUnknown periodically teams up with Twitch.tv and Amazon Prime to offer free Crates to gamers who have a paid Amazon Prime account that's linked with their free Twitch.tv account. These Twitch Prime Crates are each made available for a limited time. For more information about Twitch Prime Crates, visit: www.twitch.tv/prime.

Coupons can also be acquired and then exchanged for a different collection of items that are not sold in the Store.

At any given time when playing *PUBG*, one current Survivor Pass is sold. These include access to exclusive rewards, the ability to unlock skins, items, and Emotes by completing special missions, and the ability to earn bonus XP and BP that'll allow your soldier to level up faster. Purchasing Survivor Passes is optional.

YOU DON'T NEED TO LOOK GOOD TO WIN MATCHES

Sure, you can invest a lot of time and money to make your soldier look unique, ultra-menacing, comical, or badass, but ultimately, this is optional and has no impact whatsoever on your soldier's strength, speed, or capabilities during a match. Yet, making your soldier stand out based on their appearance is one of the most popular features of *PUBG*, and something that gamers at all skill levels take very seriously.

Any items you purchase or acquire are yours to keep permanently within your *PUBG* account. Items you own do not expire.

Ultimately, however, if you want to give your soldier extra protection and defensive strength, during each match, make it a priority to find and collect a level 3 Vest and level 3 Helmet, along with a level 3 Backpack (so your soldier can hold more weapons, ammo, loot, and items needed to survive).

A Helmet and Vest must be found and acquired during each match. Depending on the armor's level, this determines how much damage it can take before it disappears and loses its defensive or shielding capabilities. However, you can always replace a Helmet or Vest with a new one that you find on the island, receive from a Supply Drop, or take from a defeated enemy.

As soon as you opt to pick up an armor item, such as a Helmet, your soldier will immediately wear it. If he or she is already wearing a similar item, the new armor item you pick up will replace the existing one automatically. In your haste, make sure you always upgrade armor by moving up a level instead of accidently downgrading and selecting a level 1 or level 2 Helmet when you're already wearing a level 3 Helmet, for example.

SECTION 3

OVERCOME THE UNIQUE CHALLENGES OF *PUBG'S* VARIOUS GAME-PLAY MODES

PUBG OFFERS A COLLECTION OF VASTLY DIFFERENT GAME-PLAY MODES AND settings, each of which provides a different experience during a match. The game-play mode determines whether or not you'll have a partner or squad mates as allies during a match, as well as the default viewing perspective you'll have while controlling your soldier.

Meanwhile, each island map offers different types of terrain and climates to experience, as well as a unique collection of vehicles, for example, that you can utilize to get around the island.

TAKE ADVANTAGE OF TRAINING MODE

From the main menu, select Training Mode to travel to the game's training area, where you can practice using different types of weapons, ammo, armor, vehicles, and items in a variety of shooting ranges, obstacle courses, and practice areas. Each time you visit Training Mode, you can spend up to 30 minutes there with a small group of other soldiers.

Each area of Training Mode allows you to practice different fighting, survival, and driving techniques without worrying about dying. Access the island map while in Training Mode to see a complete layout of the area and locate the distinctly different areas it offers. There's someplace in the training area to practice every fighting and survival technique you'll ultimately use during matches. For example, there's a Race Track to practice your driving skills using various vehicles.

As soon as you arrive within Training Mode, immediately start moving to the area you want to practice in and start collecting weapons, items, ammo, and armor–even before the counter reaches zero.

If you're wearing armor and your soldier gets attacked, the Helmet or Vest will eventually be destroyed and need to be replaced, just like in an actual match.

Likewise, all vehicles in Training Mode can be damaged or destroyed in the same ways they can be in regular matches. A Scooter is a great way to quickly travel around the training area.

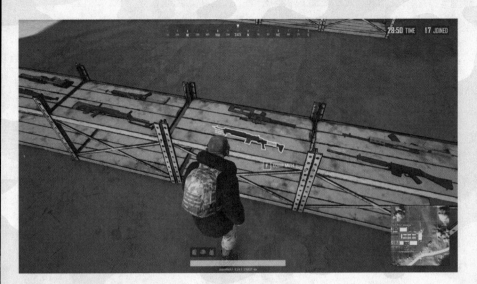

Each time new weapons or items are introduced into *PUBG*, visit Training Mode and practice using them firsthand, before relying on them during an actual match. Practice aiming, shooting, reloading, and working with each weapon.

Training Mode is also the ideal place to experiment with Weapon Attachments, to see how each impacts how a weapon performs during a firefight. Practice quickly customizing weapons with different combinations of Weapon Attachments that you find and collect. Remember, once a Weapon Attachment is found and added to your soldier's inventory, you must manually attach it to a compatible weapon in order to utilize it.

Training Mode offers several different firing ranges, so you can practice using weapons and shoot at still or moving close-range, mid-range, or long-range targets.

There's even an Urban Combat area and obstacle courses that allow you to practice fighting in and around buildings.

Be sure to visit the water region in Training Mode, called Docks, to practice swimming, driving boats, and fighting in watery terrain.

Select the Play option from the main menu and then select the Public Match option to choose between several different game-play mode options.

Click on the gear-shaped icon located above the Start button to choose between game-play modes and island maps.

From the Game Mode Select screen, first choose between the four main game-play modes–Solo, Duo, Squad, or 1-Man-Solo.

Solo mode allows you to control your one soldier in a match against up to 99 other enemy soldiers, each of which is being controlled in real time by a different gamer.

Duo mode allows you to team up with one other gamer (either an online friend whom you select or a random stranger) and then work together to defeat up to 98 other enemy soldiers during a match. All other enemy soldiers will also be teamed up with a partner.

When you experience **Squad** mode, you're able to team up with three other gamers (either online friends who you select or random strangers). The four of you will work together as allies during a match and will go up against up to 24 other teams comprised of four players each.

1-Man-Squad mode allows you to play alone during a match, but complete against squad of up to four players each. In other words, it's likely you'll experience four-against-one firefights. If you consider yourself to be a badass *PUBG* gamer, this is the game-play mode where you can truly prove yourself, since you're at a disadvantage right from the start.

After choosing a game-play mode, select **TPP** (Third-Person

Perspective) or **FPP** (First-Person Perspective) as your primary (default) viewing perspective during a match. Keep in mind, you can always switch between these two perspectives at any time.

PUBG'S ISLAND MAP OPTIONS

The final decision to make from the Game Mode Select screen is which island map your upcoming match will take place on. As of early 2019, *PUBG* featured four different island maps—**Erangel**, **Miramar**, **Sanhok**, and **Vikendi**. Periodically, PlayerUnknown introduces new maps to *PUBG* and alters existing maps. Each island map offers a vastly different layout and different types of terrain.

The Game Mode Select screen allows you to choose which island map you want to experience the upcoming match on. In the top-left corner of each map option is the approximate time you'll need to wait before entering into the desired match, based on the number of other gamers currently playing *PUBG*. As you can see, approximate wait times vary from none to several minutes.

If you want to jump into a match as quickly as possible, from the Game Mode Select option, choose the Quick Join ("?") island map option. The game will choose a location for you, based on the lowest wait time. Which island map you wind up experiencing will be a surprise that'll be revealed once you soldier enters into the pre-deployment area.

After selecting a game-play mode, default viewing perspective, and island map from the Game Mode Select screen, click on the **Confirm** button to enter into the desired match. Alternatively, click on the **Cancel** button to return to the Lobby.

EACH MAP IS VASTLY DIFFERENT

As you'll quickly discover, each map is comprised of many points of interest, along with all sorts of locations worth exploring. Some locations that contain many buildings also contain a lot of powerful weapons, ammo, armor, and loot items to collect.

Other areas offer a good selection of decent weapons, ammo, armor, and loot items, while some areas of the island will offer lower quality or weaker weapons, ammo, armor, and loot. If you go online, you'll discover enhanced maps that outline the best places on the *PUBG* maps to collect the best and most powerful items.

Two independent websites to check out to see these interactive loot maps include:

- PUBGMap.io–www.pubgmap.io
- PUBGMap.com–www.pubgmap.com

For iOS mobile devices and available from the App Store, there's also the unofficial and free *PUBG Map* app. It will help you quickly find weapons, loot, and vehicles, regardless of which gaming system you're using. This is a free app that gets updated as new maps and content get added into the game itself. A similar app is available for Android mobile device from the Google Play Store. In the search field of either the App Store or Google Play Store, type "*PUBG* Map" to find this useful app.

Remember, buildings and structures located in remote areas of the island tend to have the worst collection of items, or the weakest (level 1) armor and weapons.

GET TO KNOW THE TERRAIN

Here's a sampling of what each island map looks like. Each offers vastly different types of terrain and climates.

Erangel is approximately 8 km by 8 km in size and contains 51.47 percent land areas and 48.52 percent water areas. During a match on this island, more than 600 vehicles will typically be available, as will more than 24,000 loot spawns and 4,600 weapon spawns. Approximately 31 percent of the island is covered with dense foliage which can provide good cover.

Miramar is approximately 8 km by 8 km in size and contains 80.59 percent land areas and 19.41 percent water areas. During a match on this island, more than 450 vehicles will typically be available, as will more than 43,000 loot spawns and 7,900 weapon spawns. Approximately 33 percent of the island is covered with dense foliage which can be used for cover.

Sanhok is approximately 4 km by 4 km in size and contains 49.26 percent land areas and 50.74 percent water areas. During a match on this island, more than 195 vehicles will typically be available, as will more than 13,800 loot spawns and 4,500 weapon spawns. Approximately 43 percent of the island is covered with dense foliage which can be used for cover.

Vikendi is a snow covered region that's approximately 6 km by 6 km in size. It contains 40.29 percent land areas and 59.71 percent water and ice areas. During a match on this island, more than 330 vehicles will typically be available, as will more than 28,600 loot spawns and 5,400 weapon spawns. Approximately 7 percent of the island is covered with dense foliage which can be used for cover.

CUSTOM MATCHES GIVE YOU MORE CONTROL OVER YOUR EXPERIENCE

From the Lobby screen, select the **Custom Match** option to either create your own match scenario from scratch (and then invite other gamers to experience it), or to choose one of the pre-created but temporary game-play modes created by PlayerUnknown.

Each Custom Match that's offered offers a totally different game scenario. For example, **Zombie Mode** allows you to control your soldier as he or she tries to defeat an army of zombies.

War Mode allows your soldier to respawn during a match. During a predefined time limit, your objective is to earn as many points as possible by achieving specific objectives and racking up kills.

War Mode: Conquest divides all of the soldiers on the island into two teams and provides specific objectives that are worth points. The team with the most points at the end of the match wins.

ESports Mode allows you to complete in matches using predefined ESports Rule settings. If you plan to become a professional gamer and compete, this is the game-play mode you need to master.

Many experienced *PUBG* gamers enjoy creating their own matches from scratch. To do this, from the Custom Match menu screen, select the Create option. From the Create Match screen, first name your match, then select a game-play mode from the Select Mode column. Next, choose a Preset (related to game settings), and then from the Options column, customize the Map, Perspective, Battle Scale, Players, Team Members, and Invite Friends features to create a one-of-a-kind match that you can then experience with and against online friends and/or strangers.

PlayerUnknown continues to tweak the Custom Match options, allowing gamers to experience exiting new ways to experience *PUBG* on any of the island maps.

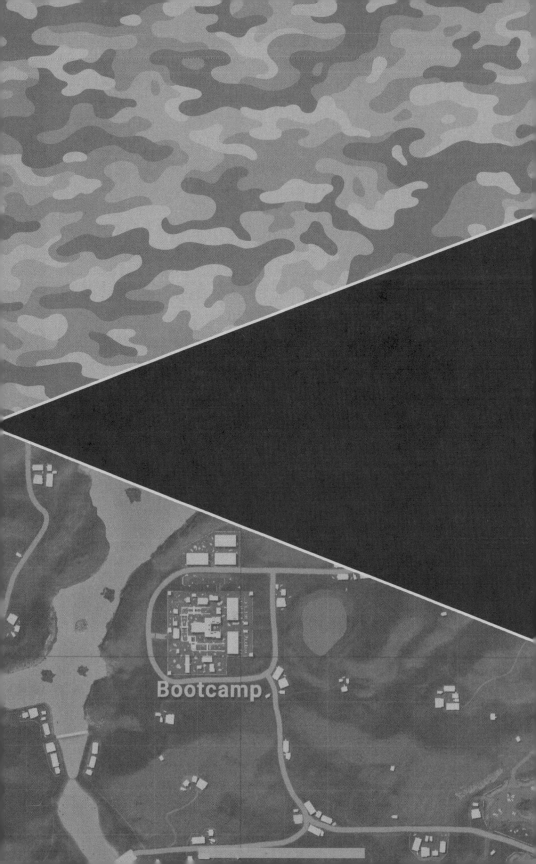

COLLECT AND MANAGE YOUR SOLDIER'S ARSENAL

AT ANY GIVEN TIME, DOZENS OF DIFFERENT WEAPONS ARE AVAILABLE ON THE island, although the selection is continuously being tweaked by PlayerUnknown as new game updates are released. Every weapon has unique stats associated with it that determine its strengths, weaknesses, and overall capabilities.

As soon as your soldier picks up a gun, immediately load it with compatible ammo, so you're ready to shoot. Never walk around with an unloaded gun. If you wait until you need to fight before loading (or reloading) a gun, you'll waste valuable time when you're being confronted by one or more enemies. You could wind up dead while waiting for your weapon to load or reload.

Notice that guns that have no ammo or that are not loaded are displayed in red in the lower-right corner of the screen where it shows which weapons your soldier is holding. When playing *PUBG* on other gaming platforms, this information is displayed elsewhere.

WAYS TO BUILD UP YOUR SOLDIER'S ARSENAL

One of the keys to success when playing *PUBG* is to quickly build up your soldier's arsenal, collect ammo, and then continuously work to improve that arsenal by collecting more powerful weapons, Weapon Attachments (also referred to as Weapon Enhancements), and compatible ammo. Examples of Weapon Attachments are: Scopes, Magazines, Muzzles, Grips, and Stocks.

Each time you hit an enemy with a bullet or injure but not kill him (or her), this is referred to as a "knock." Sometimes leaving your "knocks" alone will cause other enemies to approach and finish off the kill. When they approach, shoot and kill them as well, and then collect the loot from two or more enemies, instead of just one.

There are several ways to collect weapons and related items during a match.

As you're exploring the inside of a structure or building, you'll often find weapons and ammo lying on the ground, out in the open, that your soldier can pick up.

Anytime you kill an enemy, you have the option (if it's safe) to approach their corpse and pick up the weapons, ammo, and items the now-dead soldier was carrying.

Crate Drops are another way to quickly gather a selection of high-end gear. Randomly during a match, a crate will fall from the sky. Listen for an airplane to fly overhead during a match. Look up and you'll sometime see a crate falling from the sky that's attached to a parachute. The crate falls slowly once the parachute deploys. All soldiers in the area will see it.

Crate Drops often contain level 3 Armor and Backpacks, along with powerful weapons and useful Weapon Attachments, like Scopes. Crate Drops emit an attention-getting burst of bright red smoke once they land.

It's not always safe to approach a Crate Drop. Some gamers have their soldier hide near a Crate Drop and wait to ambush enemies as they approach them. This is a quick way to die, so always approach a Crate Drop with extreme caution.

Keep in mind that many inexperienced *PUBG* players are greedy as opposed to cautious. Thus, you can expect them to run directly toward a Crate Drop, for example, even if this means being out in the open. Doing this often makes them an easy target. Use their inexperience, greed, and stupidity to your advantage, and get those easy kills when the opportunity presents itself.

When using a keyboard/mouse combo to control your soldier in *PUBG*, be sure to memorize all of the key and button options for managing and controlling your soldier's arsenal. If you're using a keyboard/mouse combo to control your soldier on a PC, by default, the "5" key allows you to select the grenade weapon and then toss grenades that you've collected and that have been added to your arsenal.

When your soldier has multiple types of grenades, such as Frag Grenades, Smoke Grenades, Stun Grenades, or Molotov Cocktails, press the "5" key repeatedly to toggle between them. (The Xbox One and PS4 have similar controller button commands to toggle through and then toss a grenade.)

There's also a pop-up menu you can access to select and use different types of grenades during a match. Which option you choose to access grenades is a matter of personal preference, based on which you're able to access faster using the keyboard/mouse or controller you're using.

Make sure you remember which type of weapon is stored in each inventory slot, so you can quickly access the right weapon at the right time without having to guess or scroll through all of the weapons you're holding.

You may think a Crossbow is a weak and useless weapon, but with practice, you can achieve kills (even from a distance) with a single headshot, regardless of whether or not the enemy is wearing a helmet. Take advantage of Training Mode to practice using this and other weapons before needing to use them during a match. The Crossbow is also a silent weapon, so it can be used when you don't want nearby enemies to hear loud gunfire.

Like most guns available on the island, the Crossbow can be upgraded using Weapon Attachments. Shown here is the 3x Backlit Scope.

CHOOSE THE BEST FIRING MODE FOR EACH GUN

Almost every weapon allows you to manually switch between the Single Shot, Burst, or Automatic firing mode. Which you choose is a matter of personal preference. Use the Toggle Fire Mode controller button or keyboard key to switch between firing modes, when applicable, based on the weapon your soldier is currently holding.

- **Single Shot** mode shoots one bullet a time, each time you press and release a gun's trigger.
- **Burst** mode shoots two or three bullets at a time, each time the trigger button is pressed on most types of guns.
- **Automatic** firing mode activates when the trigger button/key is held down. It keeps shooting bullets from the

gun until it runs out of ammo. When using Automatic mode, the longer you hold down the trigger, the worse the weapon's aim will become, as the horizontal and vertical recoil will intensify. Some of this recoil can be counteracted using Weapon Enhancements.

TYPES OF WEAPONS *PUBG* OFFERS

All guns offered on the island fall into one of three main categories—Ranged, Assault, and Support.

A ranged weapon is one that's best suited for long-range combat and utilizes a Scope. These weapons are ideal to kill enemies from a distance, when there's a clear line of sight between your soldier and the target. Sniper Rifles (including AWM, M24, Kar98K, or Win94) or DMRs (such as MK14 EBR, SKS, Mini-14, or VSS) are examples of ranged weapons.

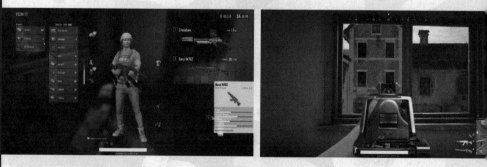

Assault weapons are less accurate than ranged weapons, but they have a faster fire rate, hold more ammo, and typically reload faster. These are better suited for mid- to close-range combat, and to launch ambushes or assaults that require fast and continuous fire. Examples of assault rifles include the Groza, AUG A3, M416, M16A4, SCAR-L, and AKM. The Beryl M762 Assault Rifle is shown here.

Different types of machine guns and shotguns fall into the Support weapon category. These are more versatile and can be used in a wide range of combat situations and have a higher DPS (Damage Per Second) rating. Some of the submachine guns available on the island include the Tommy Gun, UMP9, Vector, and Micro Uzi. Shotguns include the 512K, S686, S1897, and Sawed-Off Shotgun. The UMP9 is shown here.

Because new guns and weapons are continuously being added to *PUBG*, visit a website, such as IGN's PlayerUnknown's Battlegrounds Wiki Guide (www.ign.com/wikis/playerunknowns-battlegrounds) or GamePedia (https://pubg.gamepedia.com/Weapon _Stats_for_PLAYERUNKNOWN percent27s_BATTLEGROUNDS), to discover the most current selection of guns, and the type of ammo that's used with each.

PUBG offers several main categories of guns, including Assault Rifles (ARs), Submachine Guns (SMGs), Shotguns, Sniper Rifles, Pistols, Designated Marksman Rifles (DMRs), and Light Machine Guns (LMGs). Each weapon has its own capabilities, making it more useful in specific types of combat situations. Shown here is the M416 with several Weapon Attachments added to it.

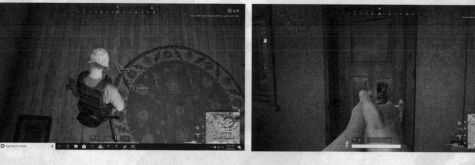

Pistols are a close-range type of weapon. Because they're the least powerful of the guns, they tend to be more useful at the start of a match, but much less useful as a match progresses. Shown here is the P92 Pistol being picked up and then used (in FFP mode).

Within each gun category, there are several distinct gun types available, although most (but not all) guns within a specific category will use the same type of ammo. It's important to learn which ammo type goes with each gun. For example, the different types of Shotguns (S12K, S686, S1897, and Sawed-Off Shotguns) all use 12-gauge shells.

Each type of gun is best used from a certain range. Some, like Pistols, are close-range weapons. Others are better suited for mid-range combat, or when your enemies are far away. Sniper Rifles or DMRs, for example, are ideal for picking off enemies from an extreme distance, especially when a powerful Scope is added to a Sniper Rifle. The AWM Sniper Rifle, for example, has a range up to 1,000 meters.

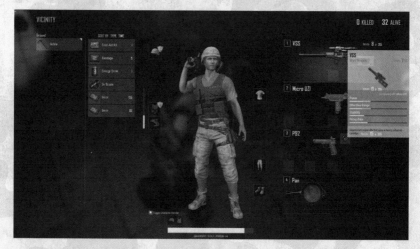

After grabbing a gun, access your soldier's Inventory screen and select that weapon to learn about its stats, along with the type of ammo it uses and how much ammo it can hold.

When you point a gun (without a Scope) at an enemy, its targeting site will be displayed. The size of the crosshairs you see matters a lot. The smaller the crosshair, the more accurate your aim will be. For example, if your soldier is in motion while shooting, the crosshair will be large, and the gun's accuracy will be lower. Shown here, you can see the crosshair near the center of the screen, within the doorway.

If the selected and active gun your soldier is using has a Scope, activate it by pressing the Aim button twice, which switches to the Scope's viewing perspective and allows you to accurately target enemies (or spy on them) from far away. Scopes come in different magnifications.

Some Scopes, like a 2x or 4x Scope, are better suited for mid-range targets as opposed to distant targets. Use a more powerful 8x or 15x Scope to aim at distant targets, as these offer the best magnification. The more powerful Scopes are more commonly used during the early to mid-stages of a match.

Toward the End Game (the end of a match), all soldiers are close together, so a 15x Scope will not be useful. Hence, you'll want to drop your more powerful Scope(s) and make sure you have a 2x or 4x Scope if your soldier survives until the End Game. Other types of Scopes, such as the Red Dot Sight are useful anytime, during any match, because it makes accurate aiming faster and easier.

Having your soldier stand still and/or crouch down will improve their aim, as will having them hold their breath while aiming a gun.

Landing a headshot when shooting at an enemy always causes the most damage. If your enemy is wearing no helmet or a low-level helmet, a single headshot will often kill your enemy. If he or she is wearing a level 3 Helmet, it can often withstand one or two direct bullet hits, but how much damage you inflict will depend on the type of gun/ammo you're using, the accuracy of your aim, and your distance from the enemy.

Whenever new weapons are introduced into *PUBG*, they're described within the Patch Notes. You can access the latest Patch Notes from the Lobby screen by clicking on the icon that's displayed near the top-right corner (PC version).

After finding and grabbing a gun, and adding it to your soldier's arsenal, access the Inventory screen and select that weapon to see its stats and link compatible Weapon Attachments to it.

Periodically, PlayerUnknown adjusts a weapon's stats in conjunction with game updates, so while it's important to understand a weapon's stats when choosing the best weapon for a specific task, don't bother trying to memorize the stats for each weapon.

Each type of gun in *PUBG* is rated based on a variety of stat categories, including:

Ammo Capacity—This determines how many rounds of ammo (bullets) a gun can hold before it needs to be reloaded. With the addition of a Weapon Attachment such as a Magazine, it's possible to dramatically increase a gun's ammo capacity. Each time a gun runs out of ammo, it'll need to be reloaded using ammo that's stored in your soldier's inventory. How long it takes to reload a weapon varies.

Ammo Type—Every gun uses a specific type of ammo. Unless you have the correct ammo for the gun you're trying to use, that weapon will be useless. Pay attention to the types of ammo you need at any given time, based on your overall arsenal, and focus on stockpiling those types of ammo. Carrying around ammo for weapons you don't possess uses up valuable space in your soldier's inventory.

Attachments—Finding and manually attaching Weapon Attachments to certain weapons greatly improves their aim, increases ammo capacity, and/or reduces recoil. Not all weapons have compatible Weapon Attachments. In some cases, individual weapons can have multiple Weapon Attachments connected to them at the same time.

Bullet Velocity—This is a measure of how fast each bullet travels once it's shot from a gun. A faster bullet velocity means you won't need to lead your shots (aim slightly in front of a moving target). This also translates to less spread and less bullet drop per shot. In addition, it means that a bullet's potential damage will diminish less when shooting from a distance.

Damage—Several factors go into calculating how much damage a weapon can cause. For example, how far the weapon is from its target, the aiming accuracy of the shot, which Weapon Attachments are being used with the weapon, and whether or not the target is wearing armor all help to determine how much damage a direct hit from a single round of ammunition (or bullet) will cause. As a general rule, a head shot always causes more damage than a body shot.

Damage Per Second—This is an approximate calculation of how much damage your weapon will do if you continuously fire at a target and achieve direct hits with each shot. This stat is more useful when evaluating a weapon's usefulness when used at close range, knowing that all (or at least most) of your shots will hit their target.

Effective Range—The distance from your target that the weapon is effective. The weapon will lose effectiveness the farther it is out of its effective range.

Fire Modes–Many guns have several firing modes. These can include Single, Auto, and Burst, however, not all guns offer each of these modes. When Single is selected, each time you press the trigger, one bullet is shot. When Auto is selected, holding down the trigger results in continuous firing until you release the trigger or run out of ammo. Burst means that each time you pull the trigger, several bullets are shot in quick succession.

Load/Reload Time–How much time it takes to reload varies greatly based on the type of weapon your using. Some guns have a quick reload time, but only hold a few rounds of ammo at once, while others hold many rounds of ammo, but take longer to reload. All of this gun-related information matters when you're engaged in an intense and time-sensitive combat situation.

Rate of Fire–This is the number of rounds (bullets) a gun will shoot per second when you hold down the trigger, as opposed to repeatedly tap it. Your weapon will continue firing until you release the trigger or run out of ammo and need to reload.

Recoil–This is the uncontrollable gun motion (the kick) that occurs when the trigger is pulled, and a weapon is shot. An aim for a weapon with a large recoil will need to be adjusted after each shot to ensure accuracy. To compensate for recoil, it's often best to tap the trigger to shoot one round at a time, as opposed to holding down the trigger (when applicable) to continuously shoot. The longer you hold down the trigger of most weapons, the more negative impact recoil will have on that weapon, causing major deterioration in aiming accuracy.

Spread–When certain types of pellet ammunition break apart after being fired, the spread is the area the pellets cover. The farther the ammunition travels before hitting its target, the wider its spread will typically be, which results in less damage. Some weapons cause a larger ammunition spread than others.

Stability—Refers to how easy a weapon is to control. It refers to the "kick" of the gun when it's fired and how much that recoil impacts aiming accuracy.

When shooting enemies from a distance, using a Sniper Rifle with a strong Scope, for example, take into account Bullet Drop. As a bullet travels a great distance, it drops a bit below the intended target seen when using the targeting crosshairs of the weapon's viewfinder/scope. To take Bullet Drop into account, you'll sometimes need to aim slightly higher.

IMPROVE A WEAPON USING WEAPON ATTACHMENTS

As important as it is to find and collect the most powerful weapons as you're exploring the island and preparing for combat, it's equally important (especially once you reach beyond the midpoint of a match) to equip your most powerful weapons with Weapon Attachments.

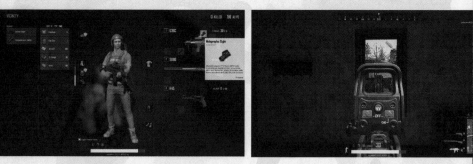

Weapon Attachments, like the Holographic Sight, can be found on the island and collected within your inventory. However, from your soldier's Inventory screen it's necessary to manually connect a Weapon Enhancement to a compatible weapon in order to make use of it.

Muzzle Attachments are one type of Weapon Enhancement. For pump and double-barrel shotguns, a Muzzle Attachment is called a Choke. This keeps the bullet fragments (pellets) from each shot from spreading out too much, so each shot focuses in on a smaller target area, thus causing more damage.

Assault Rifles, Sniper Rifles, and SMGs, for example, can use a Compensator. This controls the weapon's recoil and helps you maintain more accurate aim when taking multiple shots in quick succession.

Flash Hiders work with specific types of weapons and when attached to a gun that's being shot, hides its muzzle flash. This makes it harder for your enemy to visually see where an attack is coming from. However, they can often hear from which direction bullets are approaching from.

Flash Hiders work great with Sniper Rifles and Assault Rifles when being used from a distance from your opponent. When you're hiding in a bush or using some other type of cover, and don't want your enemies to be able to determine the exact location where you're perched and shooting from, a Flash Hider is useful. It can also reduce the weapon's recoil.

In general, you always want to have a compatible Muzzle Weapon Enhancement attached to the gun you're using. One of the more popular types of Muzzles is a Suppressor. Many types of guns have Suppressors available for them. It both hides the flash from the gun when it's shot and serves to reduce the weapon's recoil. Reducing recoil improves shooting accuracy. Shown here, a Suppressor for an SMG has been added to this UMP9 Submachine Gun.

In many cases, the Suppressor also eliminates the "bang" (the firing sound and the bullet echo) heard from each shot, which makes it that much harder for an enemy to figure out where you're shooting from if you're not in their direct line of sight.

Grips or Stocks (also known as Under Barrel Attachments) reduce horizontal and/or vertical recoil, depending on the type of grip that's attached to the compatible weapon.

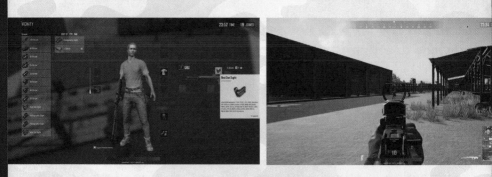

In addition to various Scope magnifications, there are different types of sights that allow you to see different details when looking through the Scope. Not all Scopes work with all guns, however. Some of the Scopes, such as a Holographic Sight and Red Dot Sight (shown here) make it easier to target your enemies. In this case, just point the red dot at your target and fire.

You'll also discover Scopes that improve your ability to zoom in on your enemies from a distance. There's a 2x magnification Scope, as well as a 4x magnification Scope (which is the most versatile when at mid- or long-range from your enemy). The 8x Scope is ideal for single-shot Assault Rifles as well as many types of Sniper Rifles.

When you're very far away from an enemy and using an 8x Scope, for example, you will experience some bullet drop. This means that the bullet will land a bit lower than where you aim in your sight, so it's important to compensate for this based on the weapon you're using and the distance you are from your enemy.

One of the "crate-only" Scopes is a 15x magnification. This means you can only obtain this type of powerful Scope by discovering it within a crate or by killing an enemy that's carrying one. This is the Scope you'll use for taking extremely long-range shots that require superior accuracy. It's the least versatile of the Scopes, however.

During the late stages of a match, the more powerful Scopes are much less useful, because as the circle shrinks, you and your enemies are forced closer and closer together, so there's little need for a long-range weapon.

As you prepare for the late stages of a match, make sure you have a lower-intensity Scope, such as a red dot, 2x, or 4x Scope at your disposal. This will be more useful than an 8x or 15x Scope.

Yet another type of Weapon Enhancement available within *PUBG* are called Stocks. This add-on to a weapon helps to improve its accuracy and stability. Bullet Loops, which are a type of Stock, are used to shorten a compatible gun's reload time.

Magazines (also called Mags) are used to store and use more bullets within a gun without needing to reload. There are several types of Magazines, some of which also speed up a gun's reload time. The Extended Mag attachment is shown here. As you can see, it works with a variety of weapons, including the M416 Assault Rifle.

ADJUST GAME SETTINGS TO IMPROVE WEAPON HANDLING

Whether you're using a keyboard/mouse combo or a controller when playing *PUBG*, from the game's Settings menu, it's possible to customize the key or button bindings, plus adjust the sensitivity of controls.

The Settings menu offers multiple submenus, including Graphics, Control, Sound, and Gameplay. It's from the Control submenu that you can adjust the sensitivity of mouse and controller controls.

Always make small adjustments to the sensitivity settings, and then experiment with those settings. Even a tiny adjustment can make a tremendous impact over targeting/aiming or Scope sensitivity, for example. How you adjust these settings is a matter of personal preference. It's a good idea to start with the game defaults as you're developing your *PUBG* gaming skills, and then make small tweaks to the Control-related settings as you deem necessary.

PUBG Pro Settings and Gear List

PlayerUnknown's Battlegrounds is an impressive evolution of the battle royale FPS format that successfully blends survival tactics, strategy and chaos into a beautiful mix that we just can't stop playing. PUBG has also entered the competitive esports scene a while ago so we just had to research the best PUBG settings for you.

This list was created by our own team of PUBG fanatics as a great resource if you want to know which sensitivity, resolution, DPI, scoping sensitivity, or other PUBG settings your favorite pro is on right now. This list, like a crate drop falling from the sky at the perfect moment, can be an incredibly valuable resource for our fellow PUBG fans. Whether you want to get more competitive, just tweak your settings, or are unloading that new mouse, monitor or keyboard; this is the right place to get your settings dialed in.

As always, please give us a shout out on Twitter and Discord if we got any of the information wrong or you need some other of the PUBG settings fixed. This list is still a work in progress but we are updating every pubg config as fast as we can. Thank you for reading.

Search:

Team	Player	Mouse	Mouse DPI	Vertical Sens	General Sens	Targeting Sens	Iron-sight Sens	2x	3x	4x	6x	8x	15x	Monitor	Monitor HZ	GPU	Resolution	Mousepad	Keyboard	Headset
Team Liquid	Jeemzz	Logitech G305	800	1.00	30	20	20	20	20	20	20	20	20	Acer XB240H	144	GTX 1080 Ti	1728x1080	Corsair MM300	Corsair K55	HyperX Cloud II
Team Liquid	Jembty	Logitech G Pro Wireless	800	1.00	32	28	32	28	28	28	28	28	28	BenQ XL2411	144	GTX 1080 Ti	1728x1080	Zowie G-SR	Corsair K65	HyperX Cloud II
Team Liquid	Ibiza	Logitech G Pro Wireless	1,600	1.00	10	9	9	9	9	9	9	9	9	BenQ XL2411Z	144	GTX 1080	1920x1080	Zowie G-SR SE	Corsair STRAFE	HyperX Cloud II
Team Liquid	Sambty	Zowie FK1	800	1.00	47	47	47	50	50	50	50	50	50		0	GTX 1060	1408x792	HyperX FURY S Pro	Xtrfy K3	HyperX Cloud Revolver S
Team SoloMid	BreaK	Logitech G Pro Wireless	400	1.00	45	45	45	45	45	45	45	45	45	ASUS ROG Swift PG248Q	180	RTX 2080 Ti	1920x1080	Overclockers UK	Logitech G910	Audio-Technica ATH R70x
Team SoloMid	SmaK	Logitech G403	400	1.00	35	35	32	35	35	35	35	35	35	ASUS ROG Swift PG248Q	180		1920x1080	Logitech G640	Logitech G Pro Mechanical Keyboard	Logitech G533
Team SoloMid	aimPR	Logitech G403	800	1.00	33	35	30	30	33	33	33	33	33	ASUS ROG Swift PG248Q	180		1920x1080			Logitech G433
Team SoloMid St...	Viss	Logitech G703	400	1.00	45	36	36	36	36	36	36	36	36	ASUS ROG Swift PG248Q	180	GTX 1080	1920x1080		Logitech G910	Logitech G633
Team SoloMid St...	SOLIDFPS	Logitech G Pro Gaming	400	1.00	50	50	50	50	50	50	50	50	50	BenQ XL2540	240	GTX 1080	1920x1080	Logitech G640 C9	Logitech G Pro Mechanical	Logitech G433

Online, it's easy to find customized key bindings and sensitivity settings that pro *PUBG* players use. For example, check out ProSettings.net (https://prosettings.net/pubg-pro-settings-gear-list).

These settings have a lot to do with what equipment those pro gamers are using, the speed of their reflexes, and their personal game-play style. Copying another gamer's key bindings or sensitivity settings could actually be a hinderance, especially if you're using different equipment, or your gaming style or timing are different. Experiment with settings that work for you, again by making small changes to each setting and then testing the impact each change has firsthand.

THROWABLE WEAPONS

Along with the many types of guns available on the island, there are several types of throwable weapons. Keep in mind, throwable weapons can bounce off solid walls and objects, so if you toss one and it bounces back toward your soldier, the resulting impact won't be pretty.

THROWABLE WEAPON TYPE	WHAT IT'S BEST USED FOR
C4	This is an explosive hand grenade. Toss it toward enemies, and the explosion will kill or injure them, depending on how close they are to the blast.
Frag Grenades	These too are explosive weapons that can be tossed. When detonated, the shrapnel flies all around and can injure or kill anyone in the blast zone.
Molotov Cocktails	These bottles are filled with explosive liquid. When tossed, a fire is created at the landing site. The fire can injure or kill enemies, depending on how close they are to the detonation and how much time they spend engulfed in flames. This is a great weapon for luring enemies out of their hiding places.
Smoke Grenades	Toss one or more of these grenades to create a fast-forming cloud of smoke. This is best used to distract enemies and create a diversion when you're approaching to attack or need to retreat.
Stun Grenades	The boom from this weapon is designed to stun and shock enemies, making them temporarily immobile. This weapon has a blast radius of about 5 meters. A soldier caught in the blast will be blind and deaf for between 5 and 10 seconds.

CHOOSE YOUR SOLDIER'S ARSENAL BASED ON THE CURRENT SITUATION

Your soldier's "loadout" refers to their complete inventory that's being carried at any given time, including the selection of weapons at their disposal. At the beginning of a match, it's best to arm your soldier with a selection of weapons and tools that'll be useful in a wide range of fighting and defensive situations. As a match progresses and you have more specific needs, finetune your soldier's loadout based on the situations, enemies, and terrain you encounter.

Ultimately, if you're still alive for the End Game, close combat will be required, since the safe area of the island will be very small and all remaining soldiers will be forced into close proximity. In other words, ditch the long-range weapons and powerful scopes, for example, enhance your arsenal with close- to mid-range weapons, along with various types of explosive grenades you can use to lure enemies into the open and out of hiding.

An "average" *PUBG* gamer will discover that having an M416 Assault Rifle as their primary weapon and an AKM Assault Rifle as their secondary weapon, along with a Pan, a 2x Scope, 4x Scope, Extended QuickDraw, and Compensator will serve them well. Rounding out a soldier's inventory should be First Aid Kits, Painkillers, and Bandages, along with plenty of compatible ammo.

A good loadout that's ideal for defensive purposes includes the M249 Light Machine Gun and AKM Assault Rifle, or S12K Semi-Automatic 12-Gauge Shotgun. However, for close-range firefights, the Vector (Submachine Gun), UMP-9 (Submachine Gun), Groza (Assault Rifle), or AKM (Assault Rifle) will make for a good primary weapon, while an S686 (Shotgun) or S12K (Semi-Automatic 12-Gauge Shotgun), for example, is a great secondary weapon.

If your emphasis will be on long-range firefights, a good loadout for your soldier might include an AWM (Bolt Action Rifle) or Kar98K (Bolt Action Rifle) as their primary weapon, along with an M16A4 (Assault Rifle) or UMP9 (Submachine Gun) as their secondary weapon, although, this too is a matter of personal preference, which should be based partially on your skill level, fighting style, the actions of your enemies, and the terrain your soldier is currently in.

Of course, you'll want to round out your soldier's loadout with appropriate Weapon Attachments, most suitable for the weapon(s) you're using and the fighting situation you're currently in.

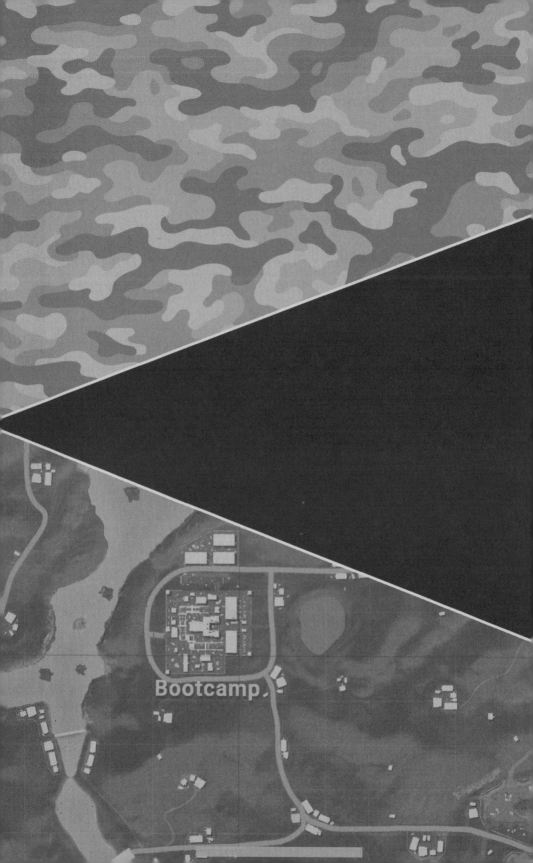

FIND AND USE THE BEST ARMOR AND HEALTH-RELATED ITEMS

ASIDE FROM A VAST ASSORTMENT OF ARMOR, GUNS, WEAPON ENHANCEMENTS, and ammo, *PUBG* offers a selection of items that can be used in combat to help your soldier stay alive longer during a match. These items are used to boost your soldier's Health meter, enhance your soldier's speed, distract an enemy, or serve as a non-gun type of explosive weapon, for example.

WHAT YOU SHOULD KNOW ABOUT ARMOR

Regardless of how you dress up your soldier and customize his or her appearance using the Customize tools built into *PUBG*, what really matters once you enter a match is what type of armor you find and provide to your soldier. Armor helps protect them against bullet wounds and some of the damaging impact of explosions, for example.

There are two main types of armor—Helmets and Vests. You'll discover several different designs of Helmets and Vests throughout the island, but what matters is their level.

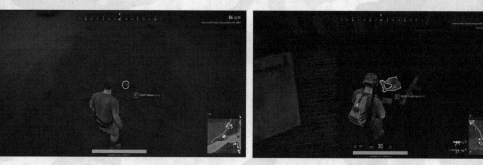

Once your soldier lands on the island, this is when you'll need to find, pick up, and opt to use different types of armor and tools that'll make your soldier able to better withstand the negative impact of attacks. There are three levels of each type of armor. The higher the level, the more protection it offers.

A **level 1** Vest or Helmet offers 30 percent damage reduction resulting from an attack or bullet hit. A **level 2** Vest or Helmet offers 40 percent damage reduction resulting from an attack or bullet hit. A **level 3** Vest or Helmet offers a 55 percent damage reduction resulting from an attack or bullet hit.

Early on during a match, you also need to find and grab a Backpack for your soldier. These too have three levels, which determines how much stuff it can hold. Shown here, a lower level Backpack is about to be switched for a level 3 Backpack.

ITEMS AVAILABLE ON THE ISLAND

While the selection of what's available to you during each match changes periodically as game updates are released, here's a summary of the more useful items that will likely be at your disposal during matches.

ITEM NAME	HOW IT'S USED	Time It Takes to Use
Med Kit	Replaces 100 percent of a soldier's Health meter. This item spawns randomly on the island (typically within buildings or structures), but they're more often found within Crate Drops. Before using a Med Kit, make sure your soldier is somewhere safe, since he or she must remain still and not use a weapon during the time it takes for the Med Kit to work.	8 Seconds
First Aid Kit	Boosts a soldier's Health meter up to 75 percent. This item is a bit less common than Bandages, but it has a greater impact on health with a single use. It's the perfect item to restore health after a battle that resulted in injury.	6 Seconds

(Continued on next page)

Bandages	Replenishes a soldier's Health meter by 10, up to a maximum up 75 (out of 100). These are the most readily available items for boosting a soldier's Health meter. Multiple Bandages can be used in quick succession.	4 Seconds
Energy Drink	Increases a soldier's Boost meter by 40.	4 Seconds
Painkillers	Increases a soldier's Boost meter by 60.	6 Seconds
Adrenaline Syringe	Found mainly in Crate Drops and rarely as loot that can be found on the map, this item replenishes a soldier's Boost meter to 100 percent. This allows your soldier to run faster and replenish their health faster, but only for a limited time.	6 Seconds
Gas Can	Quickly refill the gas tank of any drivable vehicle found on the island. The vehicle cannot be in motion when a Gas Can is used. To keep from becoming too vulnerable, it's best to gas up a vehicle before its tank runs dry. This allows you to choose where you'll stop to refuel, so you won't be a sitting duck out in the open.	3 Seconds
Cargo Drops	Also referred to as "Air Drops" or "Care Packages," these crates are dropped from aircrafts that fly overhead. Each crate contains a selection of powerful weapons, ammo, armor, Weapon Enhancements, and other useful items. You can often hear the turboprop airplanes flying overhead before the Cargo Drops are released, so pay attention. Once a Cargo Drop lands, it emits a cloud of red smoke, so it's easier to locate. As you'd expect, this smoke attracts attention from enemy soldiers, so approach with caution and watch out for snipers.	Not Applicable

Full-Body Outfits	While clothing items can be mixed and matched to customize your soldier's appearance, while armor can enhance their ability to withstand injury and damage, full-body suits provide camouflage in different types of terrain. The Ghillie suit is covered with leaves and blends in nicely with surrounding trees and bushes. The Woodland suit will help you stay hidden in forest and dense tree areas, while the Desert suit is ideal for staying out of sight in desert terrain. When visiting Vikendi, the Snow suit is white and will help keep you from being seen in snowy areas.	Not Applicable

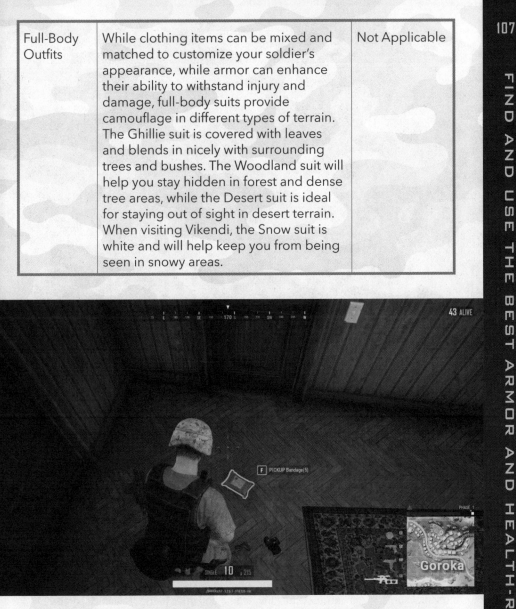

Randomly scattered throughout the island, Bandages are typically found within buildings and structures. They can also be looted from soldiers that have been killed. When you find Bandages, pick them up and add them to your soldier's inventory until they're needed.

Energy Drinks can also be found and collected while exploring the island. Keep your eyes peeled as you're searching buildings and structures, because they're often found in piles of garbage, so they're difficult to spot until you're extremely close and looking down.

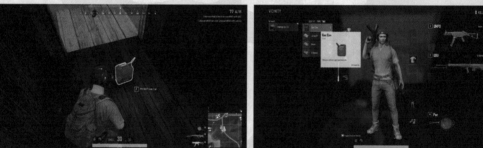

Gas Cans can often be found on the island, often in areas where there no vehicles in the immediate area. If you anticipate needing to find and drive (or ride) a vehicle, grab a Gas Can so you can fuel up the vehicle as needed. However, if you don't plan to rely on a vehicle for transportation, storing unnecessary fuel in your soldier's inventory will take up valuable space.

Because of their relatively large size, First Aid Kits are pretty easy to spot as you're searching buildings and structures, for example. Anytime you find one, grab it and store it in your soldier's inventory until it's needed. Using a First Aid Kit to replenish your soldier's health in between firefights is a really good strategy, since you want to keep his or her Health meter as full as possible.

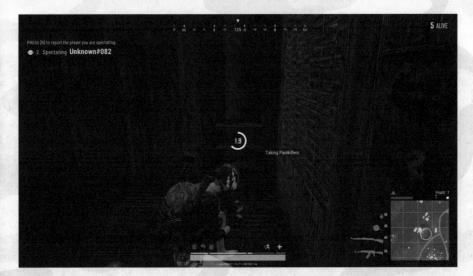

Using a Health- or Boost-related item takes several seconds, during which time your soldier is vulnerable to attack. Hide behind a solid object, such as a wall, rock, or tree to provide cover. Shown here, the soldier is within a structure hiding behind a wall. The timer displayed in the center of the screen tells you how much longer your soldier needs to remain still for the item to work. Do not move or attempt to use a weapon while the timer is ticking down or the item you're using will reset, and you'll need to start using it from scratch. This wastes valuable time.

Anytime you're using a Health- or Boost-related item, a message will appear on the screen telling you which item is being used. This is not something your enemies see. However, if they know you've been injured, an enemy will suspect you'll use a Health-replenishment item that will leave you vulnerable for a few seconds, so an experienced gamer will likely use this opportunity to attack. Shown here, the soldier is using Painkillers.

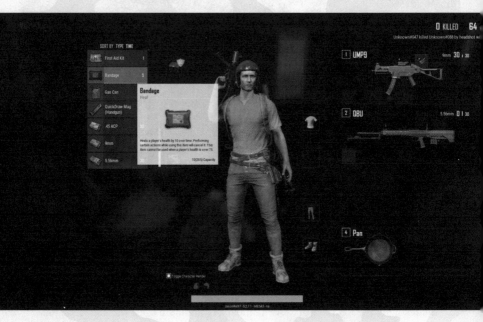

While Bandages only boost your soldier's Health meter by 10, you can use multiple Bandages in quick succession to further replenish your soldier's health (up to 75 out of 100). The more Bandages you use, the longer it'll take, so make sure you're somewhere safe.

While this soldier is lying down behind a rock, he's using the ALT Look feature to view all around him without physically moving. This is a great strategy to use to ensure it's safe before using any type of Health or Boost item that'll take several seconds to use and leave your soldier vulnerable.

BOOST ITEMS ARE DIFFERENT FROM HEALTH-REPLENISHMENT ITEMS

The concept of using Bandages, First Aid Kits, and Med Kits to replenish your soldier's Health is pretty straight forward. Many gamers, however, remain confused about how, when, and why to use Boost items, like Energy Drinks, Painkillers, and Adrenaline Syringes.

A soldier's Boost meter is divided into three sections. Filling the first section gives your soldier the ability to heal faster over time. Filling the second section temporarily increases your soldier's running speed. When the Boost meter is full, this also reduces the weapon spread of some weapons, making them more lethal, especially when used from a distance.

As you'll discover, filling and utilizing the Boost meter is useful when you need to outrun the blue wall, or enhance your soldier's overall capabilities during a battle, especially during the End Game portion of a match. If you plan to utilize your soldier's Boost meter when it's needed, be sure to stockpile Boost items as you discover them during a match.

QUICKLY AND SAFELY NAVIGATE AROUND THE ISLAND

ONE IMPORTANT SKILL YOU'LL NEED TO PRACTICE RIGHT AWAY IS SAFELY AND efficiently moving your soldier around on the island.

WAYS TO GET AROUND ON FOOT

While on foot, for example, your soldier can walk, run, tiptoe, look around, crouch, crawl, jump, climb, and swim. In general, anytime your soldier is out in the open, they should run (as opposed to walk) in an unpredictable, zigzag pattern (not a straight line). Also, keep jumping at random intervals to avoid making your soldier an easy target to hit.

Shown here, a soldier is crawling on the ground.

Sometimes, lying down behind an object, such as a tree or rock, makes you an even smaller, more difficult target to spot.

Crouching down behind an object or while walking also makes your soldier a smaller, harder-to-hit target.

Crouching within a bush offers yet another way your soldier can hide while outside.

A soldier can often swim faster underwater (shown on the right) than along the surface (shown on the left) but can only hold his or her breath for so long while submerged. Notice that when your soldier is underwater, a lungs meter appears to the right of the soldier's Health meter. If the lungs icon turns solid red, your soldier will drown. Make sure you allow him to come to the surface periodically for air.

Sometimes it's necessary to combine motions in order to achieve specific objectives. For example, you'll need to crouch and jump at the same time to climb through windows.

Peeking allows you to pop your head out from behind an object and see what's out there (or around a bend, for example), without exposing too much of your soldier's body. Leaning right or leaning left is one method of peeking.

If you're standing behind a narrow object, one useful strategy is to randomly peek right and shoot, and then peek left and shoot at your enemy. This makes it harder for your opponent to shoot back, because they don't have time to properly aim, since they don't know which side of the object your soldier will peek out from.

Another way to confuse your enemy a bit using Peek is to crouch down when peeking left or right. The result is your soldier will be lower down than your enemy might expect, so if they're aiming for a head shot and they expect your soldier to be standing, their aim will be too high.

Consider randomly peeking left and right while standing, and randomly crouch down while peeking as well to avoid being shot at, yet still get to see, aim at, and shoot your nearby enemies while taking cover behind an object and not over exposing your soldier's body.

Anytime you need to run fast, you're always better off holstering your weapon and freeing up your hands so you can achieve a faster speed. Using Boost items, such as an Energy Drink, to increase your soldier's Boost meter will temporarily increase their running speed. On the left, the soldier is running with a weapon in hand. On the right, he's running faster, because he's hands free.

TYPES OF VEHICLES ON THE ISLAND

Many vehicles you'll discover on the island are broken down, rusted, or somewhat destroyed. These can be used to hide behind if you need temporary shielding, but they can't be driven. As you explore the island, there is a growing and ever-changing selection of vehicles that can, however, be driven. These will appear in good shape and when your soldier approaches one of them, you'll see a message near the center of the screen inviting your soldier to enter the vehicle so he/she can drive it or become a passenger.

Vehicles that have spawned on the island, but that have not yet been commandeered by a soldier will always be facing east. Even if another soldier has previously driven a vehicle, your soldier can still hop in and use it, but you'll often need to kill the original driver if he's still nearby (to ensure the vehicle has been left abandoned). You may also need to refill the vehicle's gas tank, using a Gas Can from your soldier's inventory.

If a vehicle's gas tank is empty, use a Gas Can to refill it. These items can be found throughout the island and get stored within your soldier's inventory until they're needed.

The following is information about many of the types of vehicles that can be found on the island. Some are more useful when you're playing a Duo or Squad match, because they hold more than one soldier. Some also have multiple variants (meaning they look different but function the same way).

New vehicle types are periodically introduced into *PUBG* while others may be removed but could be re-introduced into the game at a later time.

VEHICLE TYPE	CAPACITY	MAXIMUM SPEED	USEFUL INFO
Buggy	2	90 to 100 km/hour	Due to its open frame, a Buggy does not offer too much shielding from incoming gun fire. It's a great all-terrain vehicle when it comes to speed and maneuverability.
Dacia 1300 Sedan	5	85 to 115 km/hour	This vehicle is not great for driving off-road, but on level roads it can reach a fast cruising speed. This vehicle is easy to disable if you shoot out more than one of its tires. You may find the horn built into this vehicle useful for summoning your partner or squad members, but you may get frustrated trying to get this vehicle to pick up enough speed to drive up a steep hill.
Jet Skis	2	Varies	These small watercrafts are great for jetting through the water and being able to outrun enemy fire. They have a smaller turn radius than speedboats, so they're more maneuverable.
Motorcycle	2 or 3	Varies	This type of vehicle allows you to maneuver quickly and works well in a wide range of terrain types. Some of the Motorcycle variants include traditional two-wheeled Motorcycles, Motorcycles with a Side Car, Tuk Tuks (Tukshais), and Scooters. Motorcycles are great for performing tricks and midair stunts.

(Continued on next page)

QUICKLY AND SAFELY NAVIGATE AROUND THE ISLAND

PG-117 Boat	5	90 km/hour	This is a fast-moving powerboat that obviously can only be used in water. Its biggest drawback is the lack of a roof, so occupants are vulnerable to long-range weapon attacks from rifles with a Scope.
Trucks & Vans		Varies	These vehicles hold the most passengers, but they're also the slowest and least maneuverable when off-roading. Trucks and Vans are better for traveling along flat terrain and paved roads.
UAZ	4	130 km/hour	This vehicle is rugged and provides good shielding, especially against small-arms attacks. It's good for off-road driving. Some of the UAZ variants include a Soft Top, Hard Top, and Armored UAZ. The Hard Top and Armored models offer the maximum level of protection against incoming gunfire.

This is a Motorbike with a Sidecar. They're harder to maneuver than a traditional Motorcycle, especially when it's carrying three passengers.

This Dune Buggy is ideal for off-road driving in the desert. It can climb steep hills, make sharp turns, and outrun many types of attacks. The drawback is that it's an open vehicle, so the driver or passengers can easily be killed by incoming gun fire. This is *PUBG*'s ultimate off-road vehicle, and probably the most fun to drive, especially on rough terrain. Practice making quick maneuvers and driving at the Buggy's top speed, since you'll need to outrun incoming attacks unless you have a passenger able to shoot back while you're driving.

Not all vehicles are ideal for all types of terrain. This multi-passenger Van, for example, is having a bitch of a time trying to climb and maneuver around rough dirt terrain and steep hills. The progress is somewhat slow, but the Van does provide some cover for its passengers from incoming gunfire. The Van has a much easier time driving along paved or flat roads and is able to achieve much faster speed on smooth terrain.

Other types of vehicles include multiple variants of trucks, sedans (passenger cars), a snow mobile (shown), and souped-up off-road vehicles. Each is capable of achieving different speeds, based on the terrain. Some offer better protection than others against bullets and explosive damage. Each vehicle handles differently (either in terms of speed or allowing its occupants to cross rough and hazardous terrain), and each works particularly well on specific types of terrain.

A sedan in the snow offers much less traction and speed that a snow mobile, for example. However, the sedan has a larger capacity if you're playing a Squad match, plus it's enclosed. This offers added protection from bullets.

As you're exploring, look for vehicles that'll help you in the situation you're in, and allow you to achieve your current objectives. For example, if you need to travel a great distance quickly, your vehicle choice will be different than if you need to climb steep mountains or cross rugged terrain and will need added protection from anticipated incoming attacks.

If you need to heal yourself, crouch or lie behind a car for cover, and then when your soldier's Health and/or Boost meter has been replenished, hop into the vehicle and drive toward your desired destination.

Depending on the vehicle, some can be disabled or destroyed with direct hits from a gun. It's easier to damage or take out other vehicles using explosives. The tires on most vehicles are their most vulnerable area, so if you shoot and destroy two tires, this is typically enough to disable a vehicle.

VEHICLE DRIVING QUICK TIPS

The following tips will help you make the best use of vehicles while exploring the island:

- Just like real-life vehicles, in-game vehicles require gasoline to function. When a vehicle runs out of gas, it comes to an abrupt halt. Since there are no gas stations on the island, as you explore, it's important to find and collect Gas Cans which can be stored in your soldier's inventory until needed (but they do take up inventory space). If you plan to use a vehicle as a way to transport your soldier around the island, keep an eye on its gas gauge, so it does not run out of fuel at an inopportune time.
- One of the quickest ways to disable a vehicle being driven by an enemy is to shoot out several of its tires. (Most vehicles can still drive with one bad tire.) However, if you want to kill the enemy and commandeer the vehicle, shoot directly at the enemy and try to avoid damaging the vehicle.
- At the start of all matches, the vehicles that are drivable on the island all start off facing in an eastward direction. If you notice a vehicle is not pointed east, this means it's already been driven, and could be damaged or low

on gas. The enemy who drove that vehicle previously could also still be nearby, waiting for you to approach the vehicle before killing you with an explosive grenade or sniper rifle, for example.

- If you're playing a Duo or Squad match, have one gamer drive a vehicle to distract your enemies and get their attention, while the second player approaches from a different direction (quietly on foot), and launches a surprise attack. Because vehicles make a lot of noise, they tend to attract a lot of attention.

- Anytime you're playing a Solo match and driving a vehicle, if someone starts shooting and you can't simply drive away quickly to avoid the incoming attack, exit your vehicle on the opposite side from where the bullets are coming from, and use your vehicle for cover. As the driver, you can't fire a weapon and drive at the same time, but you can maneuver the car into a position where it'll provide the best cover and protection once you exit the vehicle to shoot back at your attackers.

- Vehicles, including cars and motorcycles, are great for traveling across great distances quickly. However, they do take damage and act erratically when you fly over a cliff or make the vehicle go airborne, for example.

- A crashed vehicle can explode. If you drive over a cliff or directly into something and the vehicle explodes on impact while your soldier is still inside, you're toast!

- If you want to switch your active weapon, do this before exiting the vehicle to save time and to utilize the vehicle for cover while you're still inside it.

- During the late stages of any match, you're better off getting around on foot and avoiding vehicles altogether, unless you're using one of them for shielding. When the safe zone is very small, traveling in a vehicle attracts a lot of attention and offers little or no advantage, since you typically have very small areas to travel across and the travel speed a vehicle offers won't be necessary.

- Anytime you need to hide behind a vehicle for shielding, and you don't plan to drive that vehicle again, shoot out its tires. Doing this will make the vehicle lower, so it provides more complete shielding. Otherwise an enemy could shoot under the car and potentially hit you. It's also possible to punch tires to destroy them, which makes less noise than a gunshot.
- Boats are used for traveling across bodies of water (across lakes or along rivers, for example) during a match. As long as a boat is traveling in a straight line while going a top speed, your soldier can jump out safely and land in the water. However, if the boat is turning, even slightly while in motion and your soldier tries to jump out, they'll typically perish.
- Motorcycles are particularly versatile vehicles, because you can drive them across many types of terrain, up staircases, and even within buildings or larger structures. A Buggy, however, can achieve maximum speed without using a Boost, while other vehicles cannot.
- Attempting to jump out of a moving vehicle is almost always deadly. Come to a full stop before leaving a vehicle.
- Just as you should never walk or run in a straight line when traveling on foot, when driving, don't drive in a straight line. Zigzag and go in an unpredictable pattern to make your vehicle an unpredictable moving target.
- In many vehicles, you need to be going at a decent speed in order to crash through certain objects. If you're going too slow, the vehicle will simply crash into the object (and get damaged or destroyed) instead of breaking it apart and going through it.
- Whenever you're playing a Duo or Squad match as you see multiple enemies riding in the same vehicle, aim to kill the driver not the passengers. If you kill the driver first, the rest of the passengers will need to scramble a bit and become vulnerable, because they typically can't jump from a moving vehicle and survive.

- When playing a Duo or Squad match, Instead of traveling all together in a single vehicle (within a vehicle with enough seating), consider creating a convoy and traveling together in two or more vehicles. This allows your squad to split up and become two moving targets (as opposed to a single target), plus be able to launch attacks (or counterattacks) from two separate directions at once, based on the position of the vehicles. If one vehicle gets damaged, destroyed, or runs out of gas, everyone can always pile into the remaining vehicle.

PRO COMBAT TECHNIQUES THAT'LL KEEP YOU ALIVE LONGER

SURVIVING AND WINNING A *PUBG* MATCH REQUIRES YOU TO HANDLE A WIDE range of tasks simultaneously. Understanding what strategies to use and when will certainly help you achieve more kills and survive longer.

FIVE CORE STRATEGIES TO ALWAYS KEEP IN MIND

The best *PUBG* gamers keep these strategies in mind during every match:

Strategy #1—First and foremost, stay calm and clearheaded. Don't let emotion or panic force you to react in counterproductive ways, especially during firefights.

Strategy #2—Be adaptable. While you may have defined objectives during each phase of a match, be ready and able to modify your approach based on what your enemies are doing. Pay attention to your surroundings, know where your enemies are lurking, and anticipate where the next attack will likely come from.

Strategy #3—Don't take unnecessary risks. *PUBG* is as much about survival and keeping your soldier alive until the End Game as it is about killing all of the enemies you encounter. Sometimes it's better to avoid confrontation.

Strategy #4—Know your strengths as a gamer. With practice, you'll likely become better at working with certain types of weapons and achieving kills in certain fighting situations. Once you determine what you're really good at, plan your strategies around your strengths and try to avoid situations that'll allow enemies to exploit your weaknesses.

For example, if you're better using Sniper Rifles and achieving headshots from a distance, focus on using this strategy as much as possible during actual matches. As you discover your weaknesses, visit Training Mode to improve your fighting and survival skills in those areas. Practice, practice, practice!

Strategy #5—Pay attention to the terrain and avoid choke points. These are narrow locations that when passing through, cause you to be extremely vulnerable. Some choke points include many locations overhead from which an enemy can use a Sniper Rifle to attack from a distance or force you to walk directly into an ambush with nothing to hide behind for cover.

Towns, military bases, and bridges all contain potential choke points that your soldier will need to pass through safely. If you plan to go on the offensive, use chock points, such as narrow alleyways with just one entrance and exit, to your advantage.

ADDITIONAL COMBAT TECHNIQUES USED BY TOP-RANKED GAMERS

Be unpredictable. Using the same motions, actions, attacks, or defensive strategies over and over will become predictable and make you an easier target for adversaries that are paying attention. Never move in a straight line, constantly shoot from the same position, hide behind the same types of barriers, or constantly use the same "surprise" attacks, since in no time, they'll no longer be a surprise.

Regardless of where you are on the island, maintaining the high ground will almost always work to your advantage. Position your soldier above enemies so you're able to look down upon them when shooting. Climb to the top of a mountain, hill, or the roof of a structure, for example, to maintain a height advantage.

Especially when using a Sniper Rifle or a gun with a powerful Scope, choosing the best vantage point as the shooter will greatly improve your kill rate. When choosing a vantage point, position yourself where you have the clearest line of sight possible, as well as something to safely hide behind (or shield your soldier) while reloading a weapon or when there's incoming gunfire.

One way to maintain the high ground is to make your way to the top floor, or better yet, the roof of a building or structure.

Don't get greedy! For example, if you'll need to make your soldier extremely vulnerable in order to collect items from a just-killed enemy or collect the contents of a Cargo Drop, but you really don't need anything to enhance your arsenal at the moment, don't take risks or waste time collecting what you don't need.

Pay attention to the blue wall and the safe circle on the map. Make sure you leave enough time to reach safety each time the blue wall moves, knowing that the safe area of the island is about to shrink. Having to outrun the blue wall and simultaneously engage in a firefight is more often than not a formula for death. Unless you already have a vehicle that'll help you travel great distances quickly, or you know exactly where you'll locate a vehicle (and have gas for it), don't rely on using one to outrun the blue wall.

Use the blue wall to your advantage and stay close to it as the safe area shrinks. Moving toward the center of the safe circle makes you a target for all surviving soldiers in the area and often makes you easier to spot. Even if you keep your back to the blue wall, don't forget that an enemy can still sneak up from behind and launch and attack. Shown here, a soldier is on the wrong side of the blue wall and taking damage as he repositions himself.

While aiming a weapon, have your soldier hold their breath. (On a PC, press the Shift key while aiming.) This improves the aim of any gun, plus slightly enhances the zoom of a weapon without using a Scope. Remember, your soldier can only hold his or her breath for so long and it'll take a few seconds for them to recover. Keep your eye on the lungs icon displayed to the right of the Health meter, and after your soldier holds his/her breath, try to wait a few seconds before forcing them to run.

Pay attention to your soldier's Health meter and replenish it in between firefights or after sustaining damage from an explosion or fall, for example. Know what Health-replenishment items you have on hand and understand how each works. While using a Med Kit will fully replenish your soldier's Health meter, it'll take 8 seconds to use it, during which time your soldier will be vulnerable to attack, so first take cover and find a secure hiding spot.

Only replenish your Boost meter when it's needed. In other words, save your Energy Drinks and Painkillers to help you survive more intense firefights, particular during the End Game, when the extra speed, the ability to replenish your soldier's Health meter more than 75 percent, and faster healing time will be beneficial. Boost-replenishment items are harder to come across on the island than Health-related items, so collect them when you find them, but use them sparingly.

Being too aggressive during a match increases your chances of getting killed. However, simply hiding out waiting for the End Game greatly reduces the opportunity to build up a proper arsenal that'll be needed to defeat those final enemies. Choose a balance that'll keep your soldier alive, without foregoing opportunities to prepare for the End Game.

Create distractions when necessary. If your soldier gets pinned inside a structure or behind some sort of barrier, toss Smoke Grenades or other explosives in the opposite direction from where you want to go in order to mislead your enemies.

Always use your surroundings to your advantage. Vehicles, walls, trees, rocks, bushes, and other objects can be used to hide behind. Some objects in your surroundings, like bushes, will provide camouflage but no protection, while others will provide strong shielding.

Anytime you need to stay hidden, refrain from moving and be careful about the sounds your soldier generates. If you fire a gun from a hiding spot, the flash from the gun and the sound from the gunfire can easily reveal your location. Use appropriate Weapon Attachments to suppress the visible flash and sound of the weapon firing.

For close-range firefights, choose a gun that offers a high bullet capacity, so once you lure the enemy out into the open, you can kill them with a continuous reign of bullets. Use some type of explosive grenade or a Flash Grenade to lure enemies out into the open.

No matter how good of a gamer you are, you don't need to be the one doing all of the killing. Sometimes it's best to just kick back and wait. When multiple enemies are nearby, it's often beneficial to hide somewhere safe and allow them to kill each other. Once the number of enemy targets is reduced, finish off whomever remains. Remember, as soon as you start firing on one nearby enemy, the sound generated will reveal your location to everyone else who is nearby.

By having your soldier wear a full bodysuit (like a Ghillie suit, Desert suit, or Snow suit), it's easy to camouflage your soldier and literally blend in with the surroundings. Unlike other cosmetic items your soldier can wear, a full bodysuit offers a tactical advantage, but purely from a visual standpoint.

A Ghillie suit, for example, allows a soldier to blend in with trees, bushes, tall grass, and other natural surroundings within Erangel, Miramar, and Sanhok. A Desert suit allows a soldier to blend in with more desert-like surroundings, like those also found in Erangel, Miramar, and Sanhok.

Snow suits are solid white and allow a soldier to camouflage themselves in the snowy areas of Vikendi. Full bodysuits are rare. The two easiest ways to acquire one is to find one within a Cargo Drop, or to kill an enemy who already has one and take it off their corpse.

FOURTEEN ADDITIONAL SURVIVAL STRATEGIES

THE FOLLOWING ARE FOURTEEN MORE STRATEGIES THAT'LL HELP YOU BECOME an all-around better *PUBG* gamer.

STRATEGY #1—LAND AWAY FROM THE AIRPLANE'S ROUTE

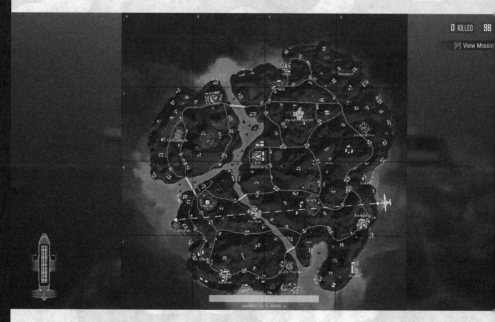

Once you see the random route the plane will take over the island, choose a landing location that's far away from that route. This will help ensure very few enemy soldiers land in the same location, allowing you extra time to safely build up your arsenal.

When choosing a landing spot, consider that you may need to travel a far distance once the blue wall starts to move, so upon landing, be on the lookout for a vehicle. Keep your soldier parallel to the land to reduce descent speed, so you can glide across greater distances. In this case, the selected landing location was the Quarry.

Opting to open your soldier's parachute extra early also gives you more navigational control and the ability to dramatically slow down descent, since your soldier will no longer be in free fall.

Upon landing, since you'll be in a more remote area with far fewer enemies (perhaps no enemies) nearby, take the time you need to seek out the most powerful weapons and gather plenty of compatible ammo, armor, and loot items. Pay attention to the island map, however, so you know when and where you need to travel to in order to avoid the blue wall and stay within the island's safe area. Use a vehicle to be able to outrun the blue wall as needed.

An alternate strategy is to land in a highly popular area along the airplane route. This virtually guarantees, however, that you'll encounter enemies almost immediately upon landing. Thus, reaching land as quickly as possible upon leaping from the plane, and then finding and grabbing a weapon (and ammo) become your initial priorities. Shown here, the selected landing spot was Bootcamp, almost directly below the airplane's flight path.

Within seconds after landing, the unarmed soldier encountered an enemy who reached the destination first. The enemy was already armed. Things didn't end well for the soldier who arrived late. For him, the match lasted less than a minute.

STRATEGY #2—HIDE WITHIN BUSHES, NOT BEHIND THEM

There are many objects on the island that your soldier can hide behind, like trees, rocks, and walls. However, it's possible to completely hide within a bush, crouch down, and potentially go unseen, even if enemies are nearby. If you look closely, you will see the soldier hiding within this bush.

When hiding in a bush, it's important to refrain from moving at all, or making any noise, or an enemy will spot you. Also, if it's during the End Game and your enemies can't figure out where you're hiding, it's a common strategy to shoot at the nearby bushes, or toss grenades at the bushes, to lure out enemies or kill them where they're hiding. (Use the ALT Look method to look around without moving.)

STRATEGY #3—WATCH OUT FOR OPEN DOORS

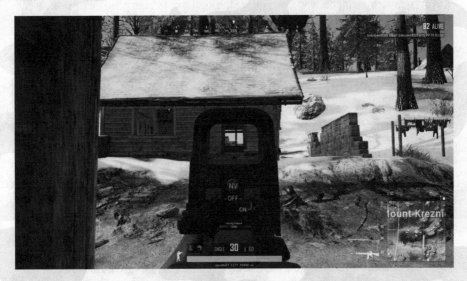

By default, at the start of a match, all doors associated with structures are closed. If you approach a structure and the door is open, this means one of two things—someone has already been there, or someone is still inside.

Try to sneak up to a structure and peek through a window or stop in your tracks when you get close to a building, stand still, and listen carefully for movement. Keep in mind, someone might be guarding the front door, waiting for an enemy to enter. Instead of going through an open door, jump through a window on another side of the structure. Peek through the window first to make sure the coast is clear, and then use the Crouch and Jump commands simultaneously to crawl through a window.

As you approach a window, you always have the option of tossing grenades inside first or shooting at enemies through a window from the outside. Remember, anytime you enter into a new building or structure, first clear it out by killing your enemies or chasing them out of the area *before* you change your focus to looting the place.

If you know an enemy is inside looting a building, grab a Sniper Rifle, find a hidden location with a clear line of sight to the door, and wait for the enemy to exit. Not only will you have a potentially easy kill, but you'll be able to collect the loot the enemy gathered while inside the structure.

Approach an open doorway from an angle, in case there's someone lurking inside waiting to ambush you.

STRATEGY #4—LEAVE LOOT TO LURE ENEMIES

When exploring a structure or building in an area where there are a bunch of enemies lurking around, always close the door behind you.

Near the entrance of a structure, for example, leave a First Aid Kit, Med Kit, Painkillers, or some other valuable item lying out in the open as bait. Hide nearby with your gun targeted on that item. Stay still, crouch down, hide behind an object, and be super quiet. When the enemy approaches the item used for bait, kill'em.

STRATEGY #5—KEEP YOUR ENEMIES GUESSING

Always try to make your enemy guess about what you'll do next. Avoid patterns in your movement or actions and be as random as possible when using peek or moving across an open area, for example.

If you're hiding behind an object, peek out and shoot at an enemy but miss the target, instead of staying behind the same object, try moving a bit to get a different vantage point, hide behind something else, and then peek out and shoot from there. Again, this will make your soldier harder to track and aim at. Anytime you get repetitive with your strategies or actions, this makes it that much easier for enemies to predict what you'll do next, prepare, and then attack accordingly.

Anytime an enemy can guess where you're going or what you're about to do, this places you at a huge disadvantage, so be spontaneous! Force an enemy to have to react to your seemingly random actions—not the other way around.

STRATEGY #6—USE GRENADES TO YOUR ADVANTAGE

Anytime you know one or more enemies are hiding behind an object in an otherwise open area, consider tossing a few explosive grenades at those enemies to inflict injury and lure them out into the open. As soon as you toss the grenades, switch to a loaded gun. As soon as the enemies show themselves, quickly shoot 'em dead. Knowing his enemy was hiding behind the rock formation, this soldier chose to light up the area with flames using a few Molotov Cocktails.

If you're stuck in a building or structure that's being invaded and you're not well armed, toss a few Smoke Grenades near the front door and then make your way out a back door or through a nearby window while the enemy is distracted and can't see you. Smoke Grenades can provide a great diversion.

Grenades are also useful when you're rushing an area where you know an enemy is hiding. As you're running toward the location (especially if you're out in the open), toss a few grenades to cause some disruptive and distracting explosions, and then quickly switch to a gun as you get closer, so your able to shoot at the enemies that are hopefully a bit surprised and disoriented from the preceding blasts.

Frag Grenades are explosive weapons and can injure or kill an enemy. Smoke Grenades can be used for cover, or to distract an enemy. Stun Grenades create a bang and burst of light that temporarily blinds enemies for up to 10 seconds. A Molotov Cocktail erupts into flames that can burn your enemies. Figure out what you want to do, and then choose the type of grenade that'll work best to achieve your objective.

STRATEGY #7—USE POWERFUL SCOPES AS BINOCULARS

Knowing where your enemies are is essential. If you have a gun with a powerful Scope attached, use that Scope as binoculars to spot enemies at a great distance. Even if you're limited on ammo for that gun, simply knowing where your enemies are hiding while they're far away gives you the opportunity to plan an attack based on the weapons and ammo you have available. You can always move in closer, toss an explosive weapon to lure an enemy out into the open, or reposition yourself to a location that's better suited for sniping.

STRATEGY #8—PUT AWAY YOUR WEAPON WHEN RUNNING

If you need to cover a lot of territory quickly while traveling on foot, your soldier will be able to run faster if he or she holsters their weapon, as opposed to carrying it. The drawback to this strategy is that it takes longer to draw, aim, load, and shoot a gun if you suddenly find yourself under attack and need to shoot back. Drinking an Energy Drink is another way to temporarily boost your soldier's running speed.

Your soldier will be able to draw their Pistol faster than other types of weapons that have been stored while they're running. If you anticipate needing to run great distances, and achieving top speed is essential, consider carrying a Pistol so you can access it quickly if needed.

During the late stages of a match, you're better off keeping an Assault Rifle (set to Auto Fire) in hand when running around, since you're very likely to encounter well-armed enemies and will need to attack quickly.

STRATEGY #9—MANAGE YOUR INVENTORY, DON'T JUST COLLECT IT

Finding and collecting weapons, ammo, armor, Weapon Enhancements, and other items is an important element of *PUBG*. However, it's important to properly manage your inventory, as opposed to simply grabbing and collecting everything you encounter.

Manage your soldier's inventory from the Inventory screen, but make sure your soldier is in a secure location before you switch to this screen and take your attention away from what's happening around you during a match.

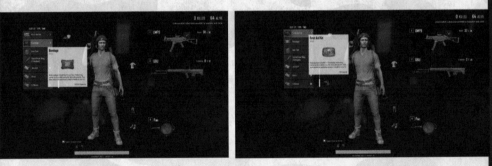

Knowing that the longer you survive during a match, the greater your chances are of encountering enemies that you'll need to fight, always keep an ample supply of Health-replenishment items (Bandages, First Aid Kits, and Med Kits) with you.

To free up as much inventory space as possible, attach Weapon Enhancements you collect to compatible weapons you're carrying, and only carry around items you believe you'll need as you go further in the match. Drop items you no longer need.

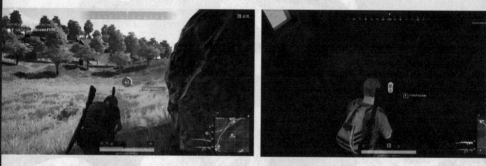

Energy Drinks and Painkillers are important items to have during the later stages of a match to help you move faster and stay alive longer, so be sure you have room for them in your inventory.

Be sure you collect and carry an ample supply of ammunition for your most powerful weapons and the weapons that you're most proficient at using. Carrying too much ammo for less powerful weapons, for example, takes away from the inventory space you'll need for medical supplies and health items.

Grabbing and wearing a level 3 Backpack increases the amount of inventory you can carry, so it's always beneficial to grab and upgrade to a level 3 Backpack as soon as you encounter one.

Once you drop and dispose of any weaker weapons you no longer want or need, drop the ammo you have for that weapon as well. Doing this will free up more inventory space so your soldier can carry more ammo for the weapons you deem the most useful or most powerful.

STRATEGY #10—PAY ATTENTION TO YOUR SOLDIER'S BOOST BAR

Located directly above your soldier's Health bar, when applicable, is their Boost bar. This yellow bar has four sections. Using Painkillers and Energy Drinks, for example, will fill your soldier's Boost bar. Adding to your soldier's Boost bar allows them run and heal faster.

The first two lines of the Boost bar allow your soldier to heal faster, while the third line temporarily increases your soldier's running speed.

STRATEGY #11—SNIPE AT ENEMIES THAT APPROACH A CRATE DROP

Anytime you see a Crate Drop, get close to its anticipated landing spot and hide—preferably at a location that's higher up than where the crate lands. Use a Sniper Rifle or weapon with a Scope to pick off any enemy soldiers that approach the crate once it lands. Then, once the area is clear, collect what you can from the fallen soldier(s) as well as from the crate itself.

Crate Drops are dropped randomly and always contain the best and most powerful guns, armor, and Weapon Enhancements within them. The problem is that Crate Drops attract a lot of attention, because all surviving soldiers typically want what's within them. If you're a newb, you're better off leaving Crate Drops alone, because you'll typically need to fight at least one enemy (sometimes several) in order to get away alive with the items the Crate Drop contains.

The best Sniper Rifle in the game (the AWM), along with the M249 (a light machine gun), and Tommy Gun (an SMG), are among the guns that can only be found within crates. You'll also discover level 3 Armor within Crate Drops, as well as Adrenaline Syringes (which are another Crate Drop exclusive). These take 10 seconds to work but increase your soldier's Boost meter to 100 percent.

STRATEGY #12—BE CAREFUL WHEN HIDING IN TALL GRASSY AREAS

Lying flat on the grass offers a way to keep your soldier from being seen, plus makes him or her a harder target to hit, especially from a distance. In this case, the soldier is moving parallel to the open road, while staying out of sight when approaching the buildings ahead. Running along the road would have made him an easy target. Crawling, however, is a lot slower than running. In many situations, you'll need to decide whether you want to save valuable time and risk being seem, or go extra slow and avoid detection.

As you can see here, lying flat in the grass while wearing a full bodysuit that matches the surrounding terrain makes a soldier almost invisible.

If you have your game's display resolution set higher than your opponent's, the density of the tall grass will appear to you more robust than it actually is. In other words, your opponent might not see the lushness of the grass and easily be able to spot you trying to hide. Tall grass also offers absolutely no shielding from bullets or explosions. For shielding, hide behind a tree, rock, wall, vehicle, or another solid object.

STRATEGY #13—LOOT AFTER A KILL (WHEN IT'S SAFE)

Especially once you've reached the midway point of a match or later, anytime you kill an enemy (or someone else makes a kill and leaves the corpse behind), when it's safe, approach the corpse and loot the dead soldier's crate.

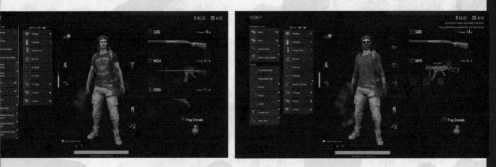

Assuming you have a minute or two without enemy interruption, check out the contents of the dead soldier's crate and figure out what items, weapons, and ammo you want to grab. Not only can you quickly improve your arsenal, you can also change up your soldier's appearance for the remainder of the match.

STRATEGY #14—BEWARE OF BRIDGES

Sometimes crossing bridges is necessary. However, this often means being out in the open and vulnerable to a long-range attack. When possible, consider swimming across a river and staying underwater as long as possible in order to avoid bridges.

If crossing a bridge is a must, use whatever objects are in your path for cover and proceed with caution. Try to stay low and move quickly.

PROVEN STRATEGIES FOR DUO AND SQUAD MATCHES

BY CHOOSING EITHER A DUO OR SQUAD MATCH, YOU'RE ABLE TO EXPERIENCE *PUBG* in an entirely different way—with one to four allies helping you to defeat the enemy soldiers on the island. If you're thinking that having some help would make participating in a massive killing spree easier, think again! When you experience a Duo or Squad match, you'll take on additional challenges and responsibilities.

To participate in a Duo or Squad match, from the Lobby screen, select the Public Match option. Next, click on the gear-shaped Options icon displayed near the Start button to select a game-play mode.

From the Game Mode Select menu, choose either Duo or Squad, and then choose either the Quick Join (?) option or select which island map you want to visit. Quick Join randomly selects which island map you'll experience. Click the Confirm button to continue.

FRIENDS VERSUS STRANGERS

Before starting the match, you have one more important decision—whether you want to play with random gamers (strangers), or a partner/squad mates that you select from your online friends. To be teamed up with a random partner or team members, click on the Start button.

You'll meet your new allies and be able to communicate with them for the first time within the pre-deployment area.

To invite a specific gamer to be your partner (or three gamers to be your squad mates), from the Lobby screen, one at a time, click on the "+" icons in the lower-right corner of the screen to send invitations.

Each time you click on a "+" icon, a list of your online friends is displayed. Make sure you select Online so you can see who is available. Next, click on the "+" sign associated with a gamer you want to invite.

THE ADVANTAGE OF TEAMING UP WITH ONLINE FRIENDS

The biggest advantage to teaming up with online friends is that you likely already know the strengths and weaknesses of each person, and if you've played *PUBG* with them in the past, you'll already have practice communicating and working with them in-game.

The more practice you have working with your allies, the easier it'll be implementing well-coordinated and perfectly timed strategies, plus you'll have an easier time making intelligent decisions when it comes to assigning tasks and responsibilities to your partner or squad mates, based on what each gamer is best at when playing *PUBG*.

THE PROS AND CONS OF TEAMING UP WITH STRANGERS

Anytime you opt to team up with strangers, you'll need to quickly determine their strengths and weaknesses as gamers (or take their word for what they're good at), and then assign tasks and responsibilities to each person. If the gamers you're teamed up with aren't as skilled as you, you'll wind up needing to help them a lot during a match, which can become frustrating.

Another potential drawback is that your allies may not have a gaming headset, so communicating with them in-game will be much more of a challenge, since you'll need to rely on Emotes and body language to exchange key information. This makes it much harder to coordinate offensive and defense strategies as well as coordinated attacks.

On the plus side, when you're teamed up with skilled gamers, you can learn from them, benefit from their experience, and will have an easier time pummeling the competition.

START DEVELOPING STRATEGIES WITHIN THE PRE-DEPLOYMENT AREA

As soon as all of your allies reach the pre-deployment area, start communicating and planning an overall strategy. Start by choosing and marking your landing location, and make sure everyone is on the same page. The key to working successfully with a partner or squad is to function as a cohesive unit.

If you wind up landing far away from each other on the island and don't pursue the same objectives, you'll quickly find yourself at a disadvantage and make yourself a much easier target to kill.

As the aircraft flies over the island, each player must choose the ideal time to leap from the plane and free fall toward land. Notice the seat layout of the airplane in the bottom-left corner of the screen. At the start of the flight, all seats are full and displayed in yellow. When soldiers begin jumping off the airplane, their seats will be vacated. This too is displayed on the seating chart. Keep an eye on this display to inform you when the majority of your enemies (as well as your allies) are leaving the aircraft.

Remember, when selecting a Duo or Squad match, everyone participating in that match will have a partner or squad. If you wind up getting separated from yours, you could easily find yourself having to defend yourself against a coordinated and simultaneous attack from two or four enemies.

Upon reaching the pre-deployment area, details about your partner or squad mates will be displayed on the screen, and assuming everyone has a gaming headset, you'll be able to talk to them. Notice that the screenname for your partner (or squad mates) is displayed on the screen, and that each gamer is assigned a color.

Anytime you're playing with strangers, you'll likely have an easier time referring to others by their assigned color, as opposed to their screenname. This requires less time, and you don't need to learn each person's name.

While in the pre-deployment area, or anytime during a match, the location of your partner or squad mates is displayed using colored icon(s) on the island map. You're also able to place markers on the map in order to set a specific rendezvous location. Shown here, everyone in the squad has agreed to land at Paradise Resort.

COMMUNICATE CLEARLY AND CONCISELY

Avoid random chatter with your allies, particularly during fire-fights. One of the keys to success when playing a Duo or Squad match is clear and concise communication with your allies. You always want to share important information as quickly as possible.

Focus on sharing only the information that's immediately relevant. This often includes details about nearby enemies. Be sure to share the enemy's **distance**, **direction**, and **description** as quickly as possible.

When sharing direction, don't use phrases like "ahead of," "in front of," "behind," "to the left," or "to the right." Unless you know your partner or squad mates are facing the same direction as you, these directional phrases are worthless.

Instead, share directional information using the compass that's displayed near the top center of the screen. For example, say "Enemy is North, 50 meters ahead, within the house's second floor." This provides the core information needed about an enemy and their position.

Also, if you're planning on taking a specific action against an enemy, in addition to sharing the enemy's distance, direction, and description, quickly summarize and share with your partner or squad mates what you're about to do and how you're going to do it.

When you're going to push an enemy, for example, either ask your partner or squad mates to accompany you, flank the enemy from different directions, or stay back and provide cover fire, for example. Make sure everyone knows and agrees upon what they should do to successfully execute a well-coordinated and perfectly timed attack.

Be sure to inform your squad mates of actions that might leave you or them vulnerable. For example, announce when you need to reload a weapon, replenish your soldier's health, or if you're knocked out and need to be revived. If you call for help and need to be revived, be on the lookout for nearby enemies, and be sure to warn your allies of their existence and location as they approach your soldier.

ASSIGN ROLES, TASKS, AND DELEGATE RESPONSIBILITIES

As a team, you want to work in a well-coordinated way. While still in the pre-deployment area, begin assigning specific roles to each gamer, based on their skill level, experience, personal play style, and their personal preference.

Keep in mind, assigning roles to each person only works if everyone agrees to adhere to their designated responsibilities and stick together. Even if one player deviates from the plan, it could quickly and easily put everyone at a huge disadvantage.

Key roles to assign in a squad include:

Assassin—Choose the player who is best at killing for this role. Make sure they're armed with at least one Assault Rifle, plenty of compatible ammo, and the necessary Weapon Attachments to make their weapons as powerful and accurate as possible. This is the soldier who will handle the majority of the close-range fighting and take the lead when launching close- to mid-range attacks, for example.

Guard—During firefights, it's this gamer's role to protect the Assassin or Sniper, return enemy fire, and serve as a second gunman when necessary. In other situations, the guard will protect squad mates when one needs to be Revived and another is doing the reviving, or when squad mates are looting a killed enemy's corpse or Create Drop, for example. When a structure is being entered and explored, a Guard might stay near the entrance to keep enemies out while others search and loot the premises.

Scout—When an area needs to be explored, this is the soldier who will do the exploring, while the Sniper keeps their distance and maintains a clear line of sight and protects the Scout if he/she gets attacked. A Guard will also be in charge of watching the Scout's back. When exploring structures, it's typically the Scout's job to collect weapons, ammo and items, and then distribute them as needed to squad mates. While it'll often be necessary for Scouts to engage in combat, their primary role is to keep tabs on the location of enemies and keep their squad mates informed on their whereabouts.

Sniper—The gamer with the best aim and most experience using long-range weapons should be assigned this role. This is the person who will keep their distance from the action, and who must always find the best vantage points (from afar) to protect their team and shoot at enemies. This soldier should be equipped with at least one Sniper Rifle, plenty of ammo, a powerful Scope attachment, along with other compatible Weapon Attachments to make their weapons as powerful as possible. The Sniper must be able to choose perfect hiding spots and stay out of sight from enemies until they're ready to reveal their location as the shooting begins. Remember, enemies will hear a Sniper Rifle and see its flash with each shot, so once the shooting begins, their location can often be identified.

Driver—Anytime you and your teammates need to hop into a vehicle, pre-determine who will be the driver and in which seats everyone else will set. Seat assignments should correspond with each direction they'll focus on with their gun loaded and aimed, to help prevent enemy attacks while the vehicle is in motion.

Once key roles are assigned, all squad mates will need to adapt their strategies quickly, based on the current situation at hand. For example, a Scout may need to stop what they're doing to Revive an injured Guard or help ward off enemies attacking a structure where their team is camped out or currently looting.

When playing a Squad match, it sometimes makes sense to split into groups of two and separate in order to achieve a specific objective. Anytime the four squad mates separate, however, they could be at a disadvantage if an enemy squad that's still together is encountered.

At other times, it'll make more sense for all squad mates to travel together as a pack, especially when traveling in a vehicle. When traveling on foot or hiding behind an object or within a structure, everyone should stay close, but not too close. Otherwise, a single explosive attack could injure or wipe out everyone at once.

KEEP AN EYE ON YOUR SQUAD MATES' HEALTH

Especially during and immediately after firefights, keep an eye on the Health meter of your partner or squad mates. If you see someone has been injured, and it's safe to do so, it may become your responsibility to Revive them.

During a battle or attack, if you notice someone's Health meter is getting dangerously low, it often makes sense (assuming it's safe to do so) to start moving closer to that injured gamer, so you can quickly Revive them in a safe location as soon as the need arises.

When it comes to Reviving teammates, only do so when it's safe for you to approach. Anytime you Revive another soldier, both the injured soldier and your soldier will be vulnerable to attack during the Revive process, so only do this when it's safe and when you're in a protected location. Consider calling over a third squad mate to serve as a guard and watch your respective backs.

In general, your own survival should always take priority, since the goal is to be the last soldier standing at the end of a match. If you can help facilitate it so you and your partner or teammates can all survive a match, that's always better, but don't take risks that could result in your own soldier's premature demise.

HOW TO REVIVE ANOTHER SOLDIER

During a Duo or Squad match, if one or more soldiers gets critically injured (referred to as getting Knocked) and can't replenish their own Health meter using a Med Kit, First Aid Kit, or Bandages, for example, it becomes the responsibility of a partner or teammate to Revive them.

To Revive another soldier, approach them (with extreme caution) and use the Revive command on your keyboard or controller.

It's common for enemies to knock out, but not kill enemies, and then hide nearby so they're able to ambush and kill the knocked soldier, and whomever comes to Revive them—resulting in two or more kills, instead of just one. Always approach an injured soldier with extreme caution.

After Reviving a soldier, make sure he or she has Bandages, a Med Kit, or a First Aid Kit to quickly boost their Health meter. If not, be sure to share one, or that injured soldier will likely wind up in trouble again soon. Be sure to stick around and guard the soldier you just Revived, so he or she can safely use the Health-replenishment items they need.

HOW TO SHARE ITEMS

Whether or not you have assigned roles to each gamer when playing a Duo or Squad match, always collect items that you need, and that you can share with your partner or squad mates. This include weapons, ammo, Weapon Attachments, and Health/Boost-related items.

To share an item, access your soldier's Inventory screen and select what you want to share. Drop that item when your partner or squad mate is nearby so he or she can pick it up.

When it comes to sharing ammo or groups of the same item (such as Bandages), you can keep some for yourself and share a portion of what you have with others. To do this, select the item (or ammo) and choose the Split option. Choose the amount you want to share, and then select the Drop command or drag the item to the ground from the Inventory screen.

It's typically the responsibility of the Scout to collect items, ammo, and weapons, for example, that other team members might need. However, all gamers should always be on the look-out and grab whatever might be helpful to themselves or their partner/squad mates, and then share to ensure everyone goes into each firefight or battle well armed, equipped with an ample supply of ammo, and with enough Health-related items to keep them alive.

While sharing, always choose a secure location, since your focus will be on your soldier's Inventory screen, and not on what's happening around your location. You don't want enemies to sneak up and kill you as a result of choosing an unsecure location when sharing.

Anytime you're looting, don't forget that throwable grenades are always useful. Collect these and be sure to share them with your allies, so anyone can use them as a diversion, to lure enemies out of hiding, or to launch an explosive attack prior to shooting weapons. Here, the soldier has collected a bunch of Smoke Grenades from the dearly departed.

PLAN COORDINATED ATTACKS

Always assume that when you encounter enemies during a Duo or Squad match that the other teams will be in constant communication and have a plan to execute a well-coordinated attack or defensive strategy. Thus, you should always do the same. Communicate with your partner or teammates before launching an attack, or when planning a defensive strategy, so everything is done in a well-coordinated and perfectly timed manner.

CHOOSE A STRATEGY THAT'S SUITABLE FOR THE MATCH YOU'RE IN

Based on the location, challenges, and competition, choose a group-oriented strategy that's appropriate. For example, it might make sense for partners or squad mates to split up at the start of a match and land in different areas in order to build up a more powerful and diverse arsenal. Then as the match progresses, everyone can set a rendezvous location on the map using markers in order to meet up before encountering or engaging too many enemies.

Another potential strategy involves one soldier standing out in the open to attract, distract, or lure enemies to a specific location, so the rest of the squad can launch a well-coordinated ambush. If you choose this strategy, try to make sure there's only one enemy squad in the area, so you don't wind up being outgunned and having to defend yourselves from multiple sides.

Anytime you and your team are inside a structure, be sure to fortify that structure and guard it, while others explore, clear individual rooms/areas, and loot. Make sure someone is guarding the entrance and windows that an enemy can sneak into.

Consider blocking a structure's entrance (doorway) with a vehicle to slow down enemies and create an additional barrier enemies will need to get through in order to approach and enter that building.

DRESS ALIKE TO SHOWCASE TEAM UNITY

One way to put a sense of fear into your adversaries, or at least intimidate them a bit, is for your soldier to dress the same as your partner or squad mates. This is for cosmetic purposes only, but it shows that you're a team that's worked together before. It also makes each of you more easily identifiable to each other during intense firefights, which makes it easier to avoid friendly fire.

Dressing in coordinated outfits must be done before entering into a match, so it can only be done with online friends you communicate with outside of actual matches. Something as simple as everyone wearing the same shirt or hat will make each of you easier to identify as partners or squad mates during a match.

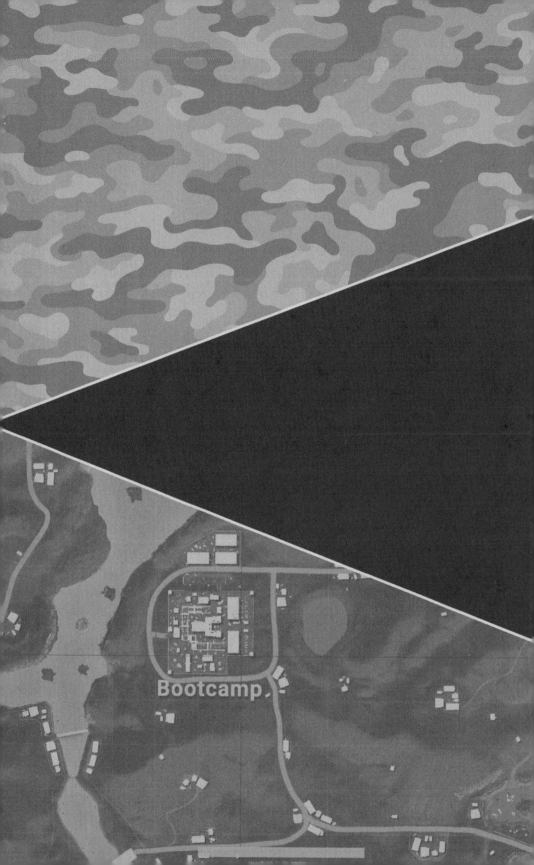

SECTION 10
PUBG ONLINE RESOURCES

ON YOUTUBE (WWW.YOUTUBE.COM), TWITCH.TV (WWW.TWITCH.TV/DIRECTORY /game/PUBG), or Facebook Watch (www.facebook.com/ watch/PUBG), in the Search field, enter the search phrase "*PUBG*" or "*PlayerUnknown Battlefields*" to discover many game-related channels, live streams, and prerecorded videos that'll help you become a better player.

USEFUL *PUBG* RESOURCES

To keep up-to-date on all of the latest *PUBG* news and updates, plus discover even more strategies, be sure to check out these online resources:

WEBSITE OR YOUTUBE CHANNEL NAME	DESCRIPTION	URL
Corsair	A gaming accessory company that offers PC- and console-based gamers a nice selection of optional keyboards, mice, headsets, gaming chairs, and controllers.	www.corsair.com
Game Informer Magazine's *PUBG* Coverage	Discover articles, reviews, and news about *PUBG* published by *Game Informer* magazine.	www.gameinformer .com (Within the Search field for this website, enter *PUBG*.)
Game Skinny Online Guides	A collection of topic-specific strategy guides related to *PUBG*.	www.gameskinny.com (Within the Search field for this website, enter *PUBG*.)
GameSpot's *PUBG* Coverage	Check out the news, reviews, and game coverage related to *PUBG* that's been published by GameSpot.	www.gamespot.com (Within the Search field for this website, enter *PUBG*.)
HyperX	A company that manufactures a selection of corded and wireless gaming headsets.	www.hyperxgaming .com/us/headsets
IGN Entertainment's *PUBG* Coverage	Check out all IGN's past and current coverage of *PUBG*.	www.ign.com (Within the Search field for this website, enter *PUBG*.)

Jason R. Rich's Website and Social Media Feeds	Share your *PUBG* gameplay strategies with this book's author and learn about his other books.	www.JasonRich.com www.PUBGGameBooks.com Twitter: @JasonRich7 Instagram: @JasonRich7
Logitech	A company that manufactures a range of keyboards, mice, and headsets. Logitech G is the brand of specialized gaming accessories the company offers.	www.logitechg.com
Microsoft's *PUBG* Webpage for Xbox One Version	The official webpage from Microsoft covering *PUBG* for the Xbox One game console.	www.xbox.com/en-US/games/playerunknowns-battlegrounds
Official *PUBG* Online Support	Get questions to commonly asked questions answered and seek out *PUBG*-related support online.	www.pubg.com/support
Official *PUBG* Website	PlayerUnknown's Official *PUBG* website.	www.pubg.com
PlayerUnknown Battlegrounds Wiki	An unofficial resource related to all things *PUBG*	http://pubg.gamepedia.com
PlayerUnknown's Official YouTube Channel for *PUBG*	The official *PUBG* YouTube channel.	www.youtube.com/pubg
PUBG Strategies	An unofficial website containing useful *PUBG* news and tips.	www.pubgstrategies.com
PUBG Tips	An unofficial webpage containing useful *PUBG* news and tips.	http://pubattlegroundstips.com
PUBGMap.io	An unofficial and independent *PUBG* website that offers detailed island maps, along with information about the game's current weapons, armor, ammo, and loot items.	http://pubgmap.io

(Continued on next page)

Razer	A company that offers a selection of gaming keyboards, mice, headsets, and specialized controllers (for PC- and console-based gaming systems).	www.razer.com
SCUF Gaming	This company offers a selection of specialty corded and wireless controllers for the Xbox One and PS4 that are used by many pro gamers.	www.scufgaming.com
Sony PlayStation's *PUBG* Webpage for the PS4	The official webpage from Sony covering *PUBG* for the PS4 game console.	www.playstation .com/en-us/games /playerunknowns -battlegrounds-ps4
Steam Community Marketplace	Buy and sell *PUBG* items on the secondary market, as opposed to the in-game *PUBG* Store (PC gamers only).	https:// steamcommunity .com/market/ search?appid=578080
The official PlayerUnknown *PUBG* Social Media Accounts	These are the social media accounts for PlayerUnknown that relate to *PUBG*.	Facebook: www .facebook.com/PUBG Twitter: www.twitter .com/PUBG Instagram: www .instagram.com/pubg
Turtle Beach Corp.	This is one of many companies that make great quality, wired or wireless (Bluetooth) gaming headsets that work with all gaming platforms.	www.turtlebeach.com

YOUR *PUBG* ADVENTURE CONTINUES . . .

As soon as you think you have what it takes to become a top-ranked *PUBG* gamer and continuously win matches, the folks at PlayerUnknown update the game and create entirely new challenges, additional game-play modes, and more original game-play experiences. *PUBG* is continuously evolving and change is always on the horizon. That's what keeps this game interesting.

Once you know what changes have recently been made, or

what game tweaks are on the horizon, absolutely nothing replaces the need to keep practicing! Take full advantage of the game's Training Mode. Plus, anytime your soldier is eliminated from a match, instead of immediately returning to the Lobby, watch the remainder of the match using Spectator Mode, so you can learn by watching other gamers.

Participating in Duo and Squad matches also provides a way to learn from other gamers, as does watching live streams of top-ranked gamers on services like YouTube, Twitch.tv, and Facebook Watch.

To keep your game-play experience fresh, don't forget to try out *PUBG*'s different Public Match game-play modes, as well as the specialty and limited-time game-play modes available by selecting the Custom Match option.

Don't let getting killed get you frustrated! Instead, focus on improving your survival time and kill count during matches, while boosting your overall rank and level. It's also worthwhile to focus on completing Missions, so you can unlock additional items and give your soldier a more personalized and unique appearance.

Most importantly, have fun experiencing everything that *PUBG* has to offer, regardless of your skill level as a gamer. Good luck and enjoy the savory chicken dinner when you're victorious!

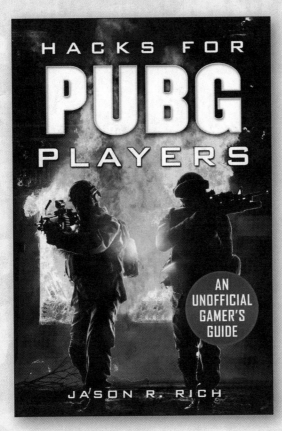

ALSO CHECK OUT SKYHORSE PUBLISHING'S
HACKS FOR FORTNITERS SERIES!